Edward Henry Bickersteth

The Reef and other Parables

Edward Henry Bickersteth

The Reef and other Parables

ISBN/EAN: 9783744762199

Printed in Europe, USA, Canada, Australia, Japan

Cover: Foto ©Lupo / pixelio.de

More available books at **www.hansebooks.com**

And Other Parables.

BY

EDWARD HENRY BICKERSTETH,

AUTHOR OF "YESTERDAY, TO-DAY, AND FOREVER."

> "Though what, if earth
> Be but the shadow of heaven, and things therein
> Each to other like, more than on earth is thought."
> *Paradise Lost.*

NEW YORK:
ROBERT CARTER AND BROTHERS,
530 BROADWAY.
1874.

TO MY YOUNG FRIENDS IN ENGLAND AND AMERICA.

THESE parables were most of them written in a home, which for long years had been one of sunshine and of song. The storms had indeed lately fallen upon us once and again; but God, who is rich in consolation, granted us a season of clear shining after rain, until, as these pages were passing through the press, a cloud of sorrow greater than any we had known before almost suddenly overshadowed us. The light of earth was darkened and the voice of laughter hushed. But you, dear friends, who are disciples in the school of Jesus, have learned at His feet that the golden glow of heaven can shine down upon our pilgrim path in the cloudy and dark day, and its melodies be heard by those who listen for them over the waves of this troublesome world. May I then venture to ask (for I set great store by the prayers of young warm hearts) that, if you find your trust and love and patience quickened by any of the stories in this little volume, you will sometimes pray that the writer and his motherless children may, in their shadowed home, see the far-off glory and catch the music of that better land, to which he has striven in every parable to lead your footsteps on.

E. H. B.

Christ Church Vicarage, Hampstead,
14 *October*, 1873.

CONTENTS.

	PAGE
THE REEF	9
AVEHDAH OR THE LOST ISLAND	35
"OVER THE HILLS HOMEWARD"	74
THE PLAGUE-STRICKEN CITY	115
EUGENE THE DEBTOR	157
PHAEDRUS AND PHILEMON	188
UNA THE BRIDE	224
BEYOND THE RIVER	272

THE REEF.

My home was situated in an island on a wooded hill, which rose far above the surge-beaten cliff, and from which, when the air was peculiarly clear, you could discern the faint outline of the opposite coast. One beautiful summer day I had threaded the zig-zag path which led down to the fisherman's cove, and was pacing the shingly shore, interspersed as it was with reaches of silver sand, when, lulled by the murmur of the waves, I fell into a muse; and, musing, my thoughts shaped themselves into the waking dream which I will relate.

I thought I was carried in spirit leagues and leagues away to a far-off rock-bound land. It was early morning. The mists of night still clung around the stern cliffs; but just emerging from their skirts, as they rolled themselves up in massive folds of vapor, I saw a little boat with a snow-white sail, and in it a sailor-boy all alone. The boat was gaily painted, and the sparkling waters fell in drops of light on either side of its prow, as the sun arose in the distant east. The boy held the rudder with a cheerful but somewhat reckless air; and I could not doubt from the direction in which he steered that he was purposing to cross the straits which separated the shore he had left from the distant mainland.

My heart misgave me when I remembered all I had heard of those dangerous straits, so often vexed with sudden squalls, so intricate with opposing currents, and so thickly set with sunken rocks and shoals and perilous sand-banks. I said to myself, how could his friends allow so young a boy to venture alone? I did not know then what I learned afterwards, that they had strictly charged him to solicit the aid of an experienced pilot, who had indeed that very morning proffered to go with him, but whom the sailor-lad, confident in his own powers, had gaily refused.

For a long while I watched the little boat, and all went well. The wind and tide at first were favorable. And I marked with joy how one, and another, and yet another dangerous spot was passed in safety by the young, unheeding voyager. At last, however, when a bold, prominent headland was cleared, the wind died away to a mere breath. The tide was now at the lowest. The sail flapped against the mast; and a strong current bore the little vessel out of its course. A shade of vexation passed over the sailor-boy's countenance; but he lowered his useless sail, and betook himself to his oars.

Now for the first time he observed that his boat had sprung a leak. It was somewhere near the keel; but with his utmost efforts he could not discover the exact spot. Perhaps he had grazed unawares some sharp sunken rock, or it might be some decayed plank admitted the oozing wave — he could not tell; but the water, though very slowly, was evidently deepening in the bottom. He tried to bale it out with a bucket which he fortunately had with him; but though this for a while abated the danger, he was soon conscious that, notwithstanding his utmost efforts, the leak was steadily gaining on him instead of his gaining on the leak. What could he do? He was already many miles from the land he had left, and he was quite sure his boat could not live to make that shore. He pressed his hands over his eyes for a few seconds in troubled thought; when his now painfully anxious ear caught the sound of breakers; and looking steadily in the direction in which his boat was drifting, he plainly saw a reef of rocks, which at low tide was left dry.

There was nothing else to be done. He continued his strenuous labor of baling. It was of no avail. The boat, water-logged as it was, was drifted by the strong current into the breakers — for you must note, though the wind had sunk, the heavy ground-swell that set upon the reef made the water broken and troubled. The tiny craft was just settling down when the boy sprang into the waves, and partly by swimming, partly by wading, not without many bruises, reached the ledge upon which, soon after, his boat was cast shivered and useless.

Hapless boy, what could he do now? A few hundred feet of barren rock were all that he could call his own; and this wretched lodgment would be covered by the advancing tide. He looked round; some timbers from the wreck of a noble vessel were firmly embedded in one cleft of the reef, and told, in language which he could read only too well, of some former terrible disaster. He thought of making a raft, and toiled long with a few old timbers, which with great difficulty he tore from the old wreck, and with the fragments of his shattered boat. But he was compelled to abandon the attempt; he lacked tools, he lacked skill, he lacked time. One hour and another passed. He became very hungry, but the only food he had was an old biscuit, which had been soaked when he cast himself into the sea, and was salt and nauseous; and, far more, he became thirsty, terribly thirsty, and there was not a drop of fresh water on the reef. He cast his eye round the horizon: not a friendly sail was to be seen: nothing but the wide waste of ocean, and the sea-gulls sweeping through the sky.

What could he do? He had been noted among his companions as a very expert swimmer for his years. And though to any one who knew those straits the attempt was perfect madness, the poor boy thought it was his only chance: — he might float or drift towards the shore: — he might be picked up by some passing vessel: — so with a heavy heart he stripped himself of his clothes and plunged into the sea on the side nearest the land from which he had started that morning so merrily. Happily for him, by the turn of the tide, the current now set dead towards the rocks. He could hardly make any way. By immense efforts he swam a few hundred yards from the reef, when he became quite exhausted, and, knowing he could not hold out much longer, he turned, and by the aid of the strong current regained, though with great difficulty, the now slippery edge of the reef, and, shaking in every limb, dressed himself once more, and laid himself down as if to die.

I think he would have died but for a sudden heavy shower of rain. It slaked his parched lips; it cooled his feverish thirst; it prevented his giving way to utter despair. Yet another precious hour had passed, and his little island of rock was almost covered with the advancing tide. Suddenly the oar of his little boat, which had been washing among the waves, floated to his feet. As a last forlorn hope he tied his red kerchief to one end of the oar, and, raising it for a signal, cried aloud for help. There was no answer but the sighing of the wind, which had now risen again, and the wild call of the sea-mew. Still he cried again and again; and, though his hands were very weary, he held up the signal of distress. But now the waves washed his feet: they covered his ankles: they rose to his knees. Seeing that the bare, gaunt framework of the wrecked vessel would afford him a little vantage-ground, he contrived to wade to it, still holding up the oar with one hand.

But the waters rose higher and higher: they reached his loins. His brave young heart failed him (I am sure my heart misgave me for him) and his brain began to reel. He raised one faint last cry:—it was a very feeble cry—but I thought I caught the words, "Save me: I perish!"—when he heard—oh, no, he could not be mistaken —he heard a man's voice, though it sounded far away. It came again and again. It nerved him to hold out a few minutes longer. And now he distinguished words bidding him cheer up and keep his head above the waters, which, with the aid of his oar, he contrived to do. And at last, for the minutes seemed hours, he saw through the mist and spray of the breakers a boat approaching, and in it his true old friend, the pilot, whose company and skill he had so madly refused in the early morning.

"Dear lad, will you come with me now?" was the only question. The friendly hand was held out to him. He grasped it with the tenacity of a drowning boy, and was dragged into the safety-boat. It did my heart good to see how tenderly the pilot nursed him. There was no frown on his brow, no harsh look in his eye, no word of reproach on his lips. He was as gentle with the poor lad as any mother could have been. He stripped him of his dripping garments: he chafed his trembling limbs: he bound up the cuts and bruises, which he had received when dashed against the sharp rocks: he wrapped him in warm and dry apparel: he gave him a cordial which seemed fresh life: he persuaded him to take some nourishing food: until the poor lad wept, and thanked him with a voice broken with gratitude, and then, quite overcome, sank into a short, delicious slumber.

He soon awoke, for the wind had freshened. And now again the pilot asked him, "Will you trust me, dear lad, now, and work our boat under me to yonder shore?" The bright eye of the saved sailor-boy flashed the answer, before the words passed his lips — "Yes, master, yes; if you'll have me."

He now looked more carefully at the boat, on board of which he thus found himself, and handled all its tackling and gear with earnest, inquisitive interest. It was built like a life-boat, being so constructed that it could not sink; and it was provided with every requisite for storm or calm, for night or day, for repairing any damage that might occur, and for taking observations of the sun or stars. There was the little anchor with its strong but slender cable; and, what the sailor-lad chiefly admired, a most beautiful compass, and in the chest beside it a roll of parchment, which was a chart accurately noting every sunken rock and reef and shoal and sand-bank, indicating the prevalent set of the currents, and marking the distances of the various tracks across the straits from shore to shore. Seeing him bending over it, the pilot took occasion to instruct and examine him in the use of this compass and chart; nor did he desist, until he found the boy could tell him how they ought to hold the rudder and shift the sail under every combination of wind and tide. Indeed, they had much close conversation together. The pilot told him how he had guided scores and scores of voyagers over these straits, not one of whom had failed of safely reaching the opposite coast. He told him also the sad story of the vessel to the wreck of which the boy had clung, and of many a noble ship which had been cast away in these perilous waters. He also spoke in most glowing words of the beauty of the further shore.

All this converse was held while they both were diligently at work, for it must not be supposed the boy all this time was idle. The pilot continually called him, as he said, to lend a hand. But it was pleasant work under such a master. For the boy could not but mark the wondrous skill with which the pilot used the rising wind, how he availed himself of the changing currents, how he avoided every rock, and threaded his way through the deceptive shallows. Many a sudden squall of wind fell on them, but the pilot always discerned indications of these gusts beforehand ; they tacked on their course, or reefed the sail, and all was well. Often it seemed to the boy the vexing squall had hastened their voyage. Indeed he himself was rapidly learning his master's art.

They had hitherto steered by a lofty mountain on the opposite coast, to which the pilot had early directed the eye of the boy. But once it chanced, though it proved only for a short half-hour, they were wrapped in the sudden mist of a sea-fog. Then the pilot closely and anxiously consulted the compass and chart — and when the fog cleared they found they had been steering quite rightly, though they had shortened sail, lest unawares they should fall among breakers.

But the sun was slowly sloping to the west ere they sighted the white cliffs, which guarded the entrance on this side and on that of the haven to which they were bound. The time seemed long to the boy, who longed to be on that shore of which the pilot had spoken such excellent things — though they were really making very good progress. However, the evening twilight fell upon them, when they were yet two or three leagues from the shore. But then the harbor lights were kindled, and a more favorable breeze than any they had had the whole voyage before sprang up and bore them swiftly on their way — and at length, though the last few waves were the roughest, to the boy's inexpressible delight they shot into the haven. They were now at rest. There were no waves in that tranquil harbor. And very soon they moored themselves with their grappling-iron to the massive pier; and the pilot himself led the boy he had rescued that day from a watery grave to a magnificent mansion, which far surpassed in its beauty and delights his fondest and most ardent anticipations.

SUCH was the parable which an old white-haired pastor, whose name was Oberlin, told to a group of his grandchildren one Sabbath evening. I must introduce you to this little circle. There was the thoughtful Aimée, a lovely girl of nearly fourteen summers; her twin brothers, the somewhat pensive Adolphe and the merry-hearted Gustave, aged twelve years; and, lastly, the blue-eyed, flaxen-haired Röschen, whose ninth birthday had been kept the day before; she was everyone's darling. Oberlin was himself of Huguenot extraction; but his son, whom God had early called to rest from his labors, had married a German lady, and she had joined her sainted husband in the presence of Jesus when her infant, the sweet Röschen, who bore her name, was barely three years old. The children, therefore, were brought up in their grandfather's home, which was on the lovely coast of South Devon, being watched, and tended, and nursed with almost a mother's care by an aged nurse, named Marie, who was as much a part of the family as any member of it. The Oberlins had, indeed, for so many generations now found a home in England that they all esteemed it their fatherland, while yet you could not but trace the irrepressible vivacity of the French character blended with the imaginative cast of German thought in the children. It had been Oberlin's custom for many years to give them a story or parable, sometimes from Holy Writ, sometimes from the "Pilgrim's Progress," or some like allegory, which he expected them to explain or prove by their Bibles, every Sunday evening And now he had promised them a new series of stories, to which they looked forward with most eager interest.

When he had finished reading "The Reef," they drew a deep breath, and one and all exclaimed, "O, grandfather, what a delightful story!"

"Well, my children," replied the old man,

with a beaming eye, "I am glad you like my tale; but can you tell me what it all means?"

"Grandfather," said Aimée, "while you were reading I could not help thinking of the prayer we all prayed for Robin's little baby [Robin, be it known, was the gardener] at the font this afternoon, that she, being received into the ark of Christ's church, might so pass the waves of this troublesome world that finally she might come to the land of everlasting life."

"I am glad you thought of those words," said Oberlin; "the figure of the voyage is just the same, though there we speak of a mighty ark, and my story told of a little boat. They are both true, only we cannot grasp all truth at one time. What do you understand, Adolphe, by the stormy straits?"

"This short life," answered Adolphe, "which separates time from eternity."

"And what you, my Röschen, by the cliffs

half hidden in mists from which the gaily-painted boat emerged?"

"The land of babyhood and childhood, I suppose," replied Röschen, "where every thing looks so large and wonderful."

"And what you, Gustave, by the sailor-boy who would set forth to cross those dangerous waters by himself?"

"Is it not one who hopes to get to heaven by himself—I mean by his own strength and wisdom?" answered Gustave. "I hope, dear grandfather, you do not look so earnestly on me as if you thought I wished to do this—once I did, but I don't now."

"No," said Oberlin, "I believe God has taught all my grandchildren now to seek and welcome the aid of the Good Pilot. But what do you think the sailor-boy's refusing the pilot's proffered assistance represents?"

The children were silent.

"Do you not think," continued Oberlin, "that when Christian parents give their babes to Jesus, as your parents gave you, in

His own covenant of baptism, as they grow out of infancy into childhood Jesus comes to their hearts — yes, comes very often — and offers to be their teacher, and guardian, and guide? Some welcome Him, but some, like the sailor-boy of our story, thoughtlessly but successfully refuse Him. But what do you understand by the boat passing safely so many dangerous spots, while it was under the shelter of the headland?"

"Is it," said Adolphe, "that we are sheltered from so many temptations here at home?"

"It is," replied Oberlin; "only remember, the time will come when you must pass from this sheltered spot to encounter the currents, and calms, and gusts, of this present evil world. What think you, however, the lad's discovery of that fatal leak somewhere near the keel of his little boat means?"

"O, surely," said Gustave, with a deeper thoughtfulness of tone than before, "the first sense of sin and of danger."

"Quite right," said Oberlin. "What, then, is the attempt to bale out the water?"

"Is it not," replied Adolphe, "the trying to overcome sin in our own might without Christ?"

"Yes, my boy," answered Oberlin. "And if so, then the boat filling with water despite all his efforts, and the poor lad being cast upon the reef, while his boat was broken up before his eyes, will show the utter failure of such struggles. Some make fatal shipwreck on this rock, like the noble vessel whose skeleton framework the boy saw. Yet you remember the hope of saving himself had not died in his bosom. First he toiled long to make a raft. This is like a poor sinner trying hard to get to heaven by his own good works. It cannot be; they will not bear the weight of his soul. He will become very hungry and thirsty like the sailor-boy, and the whole world cannot give him the bread of life or slake his feverish thirst for everlasting joy. And if he makes a last effort, stripping himself of every earthly pleasure to merit salvation, as some self-righteous ones have sought to do in every age, it will be still of no avail. If he is to be saved at last, he must be driven back to self-despair. But such experience is not gained without many painful wounds and bruises."

"Grandfather," asked little Röschen, "what is meant by the shower of rain which fell upon his parched lips? Oh! I was so glad for him."

"Well," said Oberlin, "I think God's grace often secretly keeps the soul from utterly perishing, even before the heart has found peace in Christ. It seems to me to set forth this. And what do you understand, Adolphe, by the boy tying his kerchief to the oar, and crying out for help?"

"Is it not prayer, grandfather?" answered Adolphe, "that strong prayer that goes on asking, and won't take a denial, of which you spoke to us last Sunday from Jacob's wrestling all night, who said, 'I will not let thee go except thou bless me?'"

"Quite so," replied Oberlin; "such prayer as Martin Luther said 'wrings a yea out of God's nay'—not that our Father is unwilling to give, but that he would test the sincerity of those who ask. And as at last, when the sailor-boy had given up every other hope, the voice of the pilot was heard bidding him hold on and hold out, so Jesus will surely come to those who cry after Him, even though they may have for many years refused Him. And when He comes His only question is, 'Will you trust yourself to Me and My salvation?' He will not upbraid the sinner for all the past, but will tenderly heal, and nourish, and revive him till the soul is lost in loving wonder, and sinks down to rest in His bosom."

"But, grandfather," said Adolphe, "the voyage was far from over when the boy got on board the pilot's boat. While you were reading, I guessed what so many things meant. The boat being a life-boat, which could not sink, I suppose signifies that no one who trusts in Christ can perish. Then is not the anchor hope? And the compass and chart, whose use was explained by the pilot, the Bible which Jesus opens out to us by His Holy Spirit? And the distant mountain peak by which they steered so long, a glimpse of heaven? And when this was shut out by the fog-bank, and they were driven only to the compass and chart, the Christian cleaving to the promises when all seems dark? And the pleasant talk which the pilot had with the boy regarding the voyage and the land to which they were going, our speaking to Jesus here, and hearing from Him of His Father's house and kingdom?"

"You are quite, right my boy," replied Oberlin; "I think almost every sentence of my story has some counterpart in the voyage of life. But what do you understand by the boy's working so diligently, if Jesus Christ has done all for us?"

"Oh! grandfather," said Gustave, "is it not like the text you preached on this morning:—'Work out your own salvation with fear and trembling, knowing that it is God which worketh in you to will and to do of His good pleasure?' I am sure it will be pleasant enough work with Jesus for our captain."

"Gustave is quite right," said Oberlin. "Are we not called to watch and pray, to read and learn God's Word, to fight the good fight, to take up our cross, to keep under our body, to deny ourselves, to visit the sick, and help the poor? All this will only be done and borne cheerfully, as we do and bear it for Jesus and with Jesus. But if He is with us and we with Him, then, as the pilot steered his boat safely through every toil and peril, and even availed himself of the gusts and squalls to hasten their voyage, so our Master's presence will lighten every toil, and teach us to escape dangers on the right hand and the left, and even enable us to use the troubles of time to further our heavenward course, and at last, as our martyred forefathers used to sing : —

> 'Be the day weary or be the day long,
> At length it ringeth to Evensong.'

They sighted the haven at last."

"What does it mean, dear grandfather," asked Aimée, "by the evening twilight falling on them, when they were yet two or three leagues from the shore?"

"Failing strength or advancing years," said Oberlin, with a happy, tranquil smile, "before the rest is won. But often the toil is eased at the last, and a favoring breeze bears the soul onward swiftly towards the haven. The lights on the shore are seen; and though there may be some rough waves in the saint's last illness, some sharp pain or weary struggles, the time is then very short; and soon, very soon, he will be borne into the harbor of everlasting peace, and go to the Palace Home of the King, to be with Him for ever."

AVEHDAH.

I MUST give you a story to-day from the closing chapters of Avehdah.

Avehdah — in very ancient times called Shulam — was a large and beautiful island, larger than England, and was situate in the wide ocean, many hundred miles away from the nearest continent. It was clothed with noble forests, in which grew almost every kind of fragrant and fruitful tree. It was intersected by solemn mountains, whose snowy peaks seemed to mingle with the blue heavens into which they climbed; and from the glaciers and springs of these mountains there flowed many rapid crystal rivers to the purple sea. It was altogether a delightsome land, and was owned by the mightiest monarch of the continent, who was so fond of its beauty and freshness that he designed it for a marriage portion for his only son. In the records of Avehdah this monarch is called THE KING, and his son THE PRINCE.

The island had been originally peopled by a hardy, truthful, and affectionate race. The easy tribute of fruits and spices and gems — for Avehdah abounded not only, as I said, with fruit trees, but with all aromatic shrubs, and also with precious stones — was cheerfully and punctually delivered to the royal merchants. The voice of song was heard from every home, and it seemed that the peaceful inhabitants were as happy and secure as the peerless isle in which they dwelt.

But the event proved far otherwise. For a cruel, crafty enemy of the King, a satrap who had revolted from his sway, and had already usurped a vast dominion far stretching towards the north, fixed his baleful regards on Avehdah, and determined if possible to wrest it from the sceptre of its rightful sovereign. This usurper's name was Abaddon, or "the destroyer." He knew that to accomplish his purpose would be impossible so long as the simple-hearted dwellers in that land were true to their allegiance. He therefore came over at first in disguise, with a few like-minded associates; and under pretence of trafficking in the island — by offering rich vestments of a foreign manufacture, and vessels embossed with many a strange device, in exchange for the simple produce of their gardens and vineyards — he so ingratiated himself with the people that they freely admitted him to their hearts and homes.

Abaddon was in ecstasy of delight at his

success. This, however, he carefully concealed, and only spoke of himself as one who longed to raise those among whom he was sojourning to a far higher standard of knowledge and enjoyment. And it was only very gradually, and with consummate skill, that he and his comrades began to insinuate questionings and doubts as to the wisdom and goodness of the King. "It was long, very long since their monarch had set foot on their shores." "Surely, if he cared for it so much, he would visit them more frequently." "What, after all, was his claim to the sovereignty over an isle which lay so far away from his own dominions?" "Why should they send away the choicest of their fruits and spices and jewels to a land from which they never returned?" "It is true the King spoke of his son fixing his home here; but the promise was still delayed." "Would it not be better to have a ruler of their own choice, and at once?"

These words of Abaddon sank into the

hearts of the people of Avehdah. It was all in vain that the royal merchants and collectors of tribute warned them of his true character. The islanders resented what they called base and baseless suspicions. They entered into daily closer league with their new friends; until Abaddon thought he might safely send for a larger body of his adherents. They came in troops, and brought all the munitions of war with them; but these were hidden from view in countless bales of merchandise. New tastes for foreign goods were rapidly springing up among the people.

Well, years rolled on, and still the followers of Abaddon increased in number; until, little by little, he had introduced a vast army into that island. Then at last he threw off the mask. Partly by persuasion, partly by suspicion, partly, as he waxed stronger, by threats, he induced the nobles and elders of the people to raise the standard of revolt, and to refuse any longer to pay the appointed tribute. Shortly after, by the aid of his emissaries, who were dispersed all over the land, Abaddon caused himself to be elected the governor of Avehdah. And now, to rivet his dominion more closely, he changed both times and laws. He abolished the former sacred days in which the people had rested from their easy toil, alleging that every day was alike their own, for pleasure or for work. He loosened by degrees all the ties of kinship. Children no longer cherished the same respect for their parents, nor neighbor for neighbor, nor friend for friend. "LET EVERY MAN DO WHAT IS RIGHT IN HIS OWN EYES," was proclaimed as the Magna Charta of the island. Soon worse evils forced an entrance; distrust bred faction; and faction, feuds; and feuds, violence. Deeds of rapine and of wrong were done. The soil of Avehdah was for the first time stained with the blood of murder. And now you might hear, as evening deepened into night, the cries of injured innocence from hamlets whence once ascended only the songs of overflowing joy.

These were dark days for Avehdah. For now the soldiers of Abaddon began to show themselves in their true colors. They trampled on every thing that was good. They maltreated all who opposed them. They compelled many of the islanders — women and children as well as men — to work in dark and gloomy mines, which their restless avarice discovered among the mountains. Over these miners and their families they appointed hard taskmasters. What deeds of cruelty and crime were wrought in those dark abysses of the earth I cannot and dare not tell. For the soldiers of the governor encouraged every vice, and jeered at every remnant of virtue. One thing I marked, they seemed to infuse into the bosoms of their victims their own insatiable greed of lucre.

Then it was that the royal merchants first called the island "Avehdah," which signifies in the Hebrew tongue " that which was lost;" for its former name " Shulam," or "she that is at peace," was dropped by universal consent, and never heard of more.

You must not think, however, that all this while the King was careless of the high dishonor which had been done to his authority, or to the deep miseries into which the dwellers of Avehdah had plunged themselves. He sent them messengers after messengers, who expostulated with them, sometimes in the strongest, sometimes in the tenderest terms. Nor were their warnings and entreaties altogether fruitless. Some of the islanders welcomed them, and pledged their faith anew to the King, and entered into a solemn league to oppose Abaddon and his soldiers to the uttermost. These faithful ones were few and far between compared with the teeming myriads of the revolted inhabitants; yet some were never wanting in every province, nor was their testimony ever altogether silenced.

AVEHDAH. 43

Abaddon's most strenuous efforts were directed to intercept these messengers, and to pervert, or, if he could not pervert, to destroy, those who gave heed to them. He denounced them as his enemies. He beat, he imprisoned, he put them to death. Indeed, for many long years it was a state of suppressed civil war in the unhappy island of Avehdah.

There was a time when the usurper fondly imagined he had succeeded in establishing his undisputed sway. All open opposition seemed crushed. There were secret servants of the King in all ranks, of whom Abaddon knew not, and the murmurs of serfs and groans of prisoners did not seem worth his regarding. But then (so I have read in the chronicles of the island), when he was boasting most loudly of his success, tidings were brought to his court which troubled him greatly. It was announced that the Prince, laying aside his royal estate, had landed from a little boat on the shore of Avehdah, and was himself passing quietly from home to home among his true-hearted subjects, and giving them tokens of his royal approval.

What happened at that eventful time belongs altogether to another chapter of Avehdah's story, nor must I enter on it now. Suffice it to say that the Prince met Abaddon face to face and rebuked him. And though he was afterwards seized by the rebels and soldiers and suffered foul indignities at their hands, he broke loose from the prison in which they immured him. Nor did he leave the island till he had confirmed all his faithful ones in their allegiance, and banded them together in a common covenant to fight against the usurper and his hosts in a panoply of proof, which he told them his messengers would always be ready to supply from a secret arsenal in the metropolis. Moreover, he solemnly promised them that, when he had been proclaimed as heir of the island by his father, he would return with an overwhelming army and take possession of his rightful inheritance. He said that he could not tell them exactly what day, or month, or year, he should return, for this depended on the will of his royal father and the counsel they should hold together. But he said that, when he came, he would certainly bind Abaddon and his hosts in chains from which they should never be loosed, and consign them to a penal fortress, in a far-off land, from whence they should never escape. He said, moreover, that those of the islanders who cast in their lot with Abaddon now, and refused all the messages of the royal clemency, must share the doom of the rebel satrap then; but that he himself would reward his true followers with large and lasting recompense from the boundless treasury of his father.

As aforesaid, I do not profess to give you the whole history of the wars of Avehdah. The records are very interesting; but they fill many volumes. For after the departure of the Prince the intestine war between the hosts of Abaddon on the one side, aided and abetted as they were by the revolted islanders, and the scattered but brave and ever-increasing adherents of the Prince on the other, became sharper than ever. The conflict was waged with very varying success. Now, for a while, a secluded valley would be entirely occupied by the Prince's loyal subjects, and they would persuade those on every side to embrace the same righteous cause. Then, not seldom, a legion of the usurper's soldiers would come and violently take possession of the valley, slaughtering or capturing its inhabitants. Yet it was generally observed that the flame of devotion to the Prince, if apparently crushed in one spot, burst forth anew and unexpectedly in many surrounding places. And, what is worthy of especial note, immediately after the Prince's return to his father's court, his personal friends, by dint of heroic courage, effected a lodgment in one quarter of the metropolis of Avehdah. Nor could Abaddon, with all his power and subtlety, drive them out, for they were supplied with armor from the royal arsenal, which his boldest warriors could not withstand. What rendered this of the more importance was, that quarter of the city embraced a small haven, by which continual intercourse was kept up with the King's country, and supplies received, though from time to time the cruisers of the enemy captured some of the smaller craft. But here and elsewhere many acts of dauntless intrepidity were wrought, all of which were reported by the royal merchants to the King.

Well, so years passed on. But the hearts of the Prince's servants in Avehdah grew faint and weary, and when they computed the long time that had elapsed, they hardly knew how to answer the contemptuous question which was ever on the lips of their taunting foes: "Where is the promise of his coming?" They *did* answer in his own words, for he had sent them several letters in his own handwriting and sealed with his own signet: "The time is short; he will surely come; he will not tarry;" but the reply was not seldom uttered with a trembling voice. However, after many seasons had passed and gone, vessels of war bearing the royal flag were more frequently observed on the far horizon; and the watchword, "He cometh quickly," was passed continually from one to another of his servants. Still days and weeks rolled on, and he came not. The usurper Abaddon redoubled his diligence; his troops were constantly on the alert; he kept the more daring spirits among the islanders far away from the sea-coast, and tried to wear them down with incessant labor. Howbeit, from time to time a message reached the island through the city port; and the hope of the faithful inhabitants, though it often burned low, never went out.

It was at this time (spring had given way to summer, and summer to autumn, and autumn had already passed into winter with its long nights) that a messenger of the King, with a band of true-hearted comrades clothed in armor of proof, breaking through the cordon of guards which surrounded the locality, made their perilous way in the fourth watch of the night through a deep defile of the mountains, and down a long cavernous passage, which led to a vast subterranean silver mine. There a most melancholy spectacle met their view. In that mine the miners were compelled to work in gangs or relays, day and night, so that the work never ceased. Accordingly at one spot men and women and children, all clothed in rags, might be seen hewing the rocky soil with pickaxes, or bending to the earth under heavy burdens, or smelting the ore in furnaces of suffocating heat; while often the lash of the taskmaker was heard, and the answering groan of the hapless slave. At another spot large numbers had sunk down in heavy slumber. Not far off from these a fierce dispute was raging among another group. And again a little distance off there was a large knot of miners pointing with a sad pleasure to the heaps of precious metal they had obtained.

Now, when he had gained a little vantage-ground in the midst of the mine, the messenger put a silver trumpet to his lips and blew a long and musical blast. It was strange, you may be sure, to hear such a sound in such a place. The echoes repeated themselves in the impenetrable gloom of the further recesses, and the whole cavern rang again with the unwonted strain. Most of the poor toiling laborers stood still to listen. Some of the sleepers awoke; not all, — though the associates of the messenger laid their hands upon them, and even pushed them with their staves. Those who watched the heaps of silver ore clutched the barrows in which it was piled, as if they thought some one was come to deprive them of the fruit of their toil. And most of the angry disputants stilled their quarrel, as again and yet again the blasts of the silver trumpet

reverberated through the mine. And when its latest echo died away, the voice of the messenger was distinctly heard proclaiming, *The night is far spent; the day is at hand. Cast off, therefore, the works of darkness; and put on the armor of light.*

It is impossible here to narrate all the arguments which the messenger used; how he spoke to them of their present misery and degradation; how he unmasked the hideous character of the governor Abaddon; how he charged them with the basest ingratitude in throwing off their allegiance to the best and most generous of monarchs; how he assured them that the Prince had sent this latest embassy to certify them of a free pardon for all the past, and of a place among his own followers, if they would only now receive his overtures of grace; how he set forth the high honor of being numbered with the Prince's servants and enrolled among his soldiers; and, lastly, how he told them the time for decision was short, very short, for the Prince was at hand with his father's irresistible army; but the messenger ended even as he began — *The night is far spent; the day is at hand. Cast off, therefore, the works of darkness; and put on the armor of light.*

Thereupon the messenger and his companions opened out to the wondering eyes of these poor enslaved miners chests of white apparel and of gleaming armor, which they had brought with them. And now it was a goodly sight to see one and another of these long-oppressed and degraded ones throwing down the pickaxe and shovel, casting off their miserable rags, and clothing themselves with the beautiful uniform and panoply of the King. The father encouraged the son to come, and the son the father; a brother persuaded his brother, and a friend his friend. And it was said to the women and children that there was a part for them to bear, so they likewise were clad in raiment and armor suitable to their strength and tender years.

Oh, would that all had enrolled themselves among the Prince's followers at the royal messenger's invitation that morning! But not a few replied that they had become accustomed to the mine now, and did not care to leave it. Some would not awake; though shaken and aroused, they muttered as men in a half-dream, Yet a little sleep, a little slumber, a little folding of the hands to sleep. Some answered, We will settle the matters we have in dispute with our comrades first, and will then accept this invitation. Others roundly affirmed they would never quit the heaps of silver they had so laboriously gathered. Indeed only two or three came forward from that group, and they not without many a sharp pang as they looked back on their forsaken hoards. And many, when urged again and again, replied, Go thy way for this time: to-morrow we will come; why should you think the Prince will come to-day? Come to-morrow, and we will handle that brave armor and put on that beautiful apparel. Persuasions were useless: that one word "to-morrow" blunted every appeal.

However, a goodly band of nearly a hundred souls gathered round the trumpeter, and enrolled their names in his book, and pledged themselves to fight for the Prince. These were all clad in white robes, and furnished with armor of proof. And now the messenger led them forth from the dark mine. The morning was just flushing the eastern horizon with a faint tinge of pearl. A troop of Abaddon's forces had mustered to oppose their escape, and attacked them as soon as they emerged from the cavern. More wounds were received than given, for they were unskilful in the art of sword and shield. But though it was a sore conflict for such inexperienced soldiers, the trumpet note was continually sounding — "The time is short;" and, led by the messenger and his comrades, the emancipated slaves acquitted themselves bravely, and fought their way to a small encampment of friends which was situate on a neighboring hill.

These allies, who welcomed them heartily, they found in a state of most eager joy. For no less than three couriers had arrived, in as many hours that morning, announcing that the Prince's fleet was lying off the shores of Avehdah, and that the sea, far as the eye could reach, was covered with the snowy sails of his countless vessels of war. Each courier brought a letter in the Prince's own handwriting. The first simply contained the words, " Behold, I come quickly." The second was somewhat longer, and ran thus, " Behold, I come quickly, and my reward is with me to give every man according as his work shall be." And the third was to the same effect as the first, " Surely, I come quickly;" only this courier said that he was ordered to ask for some answer to the gracious message of the Prince. So, after a short consultation, it was determined to reply in terms which might be a humble and reverent echo to his own words, "So be it: even so, come, Lord, come."

This reply, therefore, with the full consent of those so recently set free from the mine, was hastily written and despatched. All cordially consented to it; only some looked sad when they remembered how long they had served the base usurper, and how short a time they had been enrolled in the King's army, until they recalled again the messenger's assurance that all the past should be forgiven: then their countenances again grew serene and bright. And others felt grieved at heart when they thought on their companions in the mine, who had refused every entreaty. However, there was no time now to renew the invitation. Things moved on with a strange rapidity that day. For it seemed the last courier had scarcely time to reach the coast, when tidings were brought that the fleet was casting anchor in a spacious bay; and, an hour after, that the Prince himself, surrounded with a noble staff of officers, had landed. And so, indeed, it was; nor had the sun sunk beneath the western waves before his whole army was safely disembarked, and his standard raised on the shores of Avehdah.

I must not dwell on all that followed; how the hosts of Abaddon, after a faint, ineffectual resistance, fled, overwhelmed with terror; how the usurper was taken captive in the midst of his stricken followers, and loaded with chains; how the whole land was subdued under the sceptre of the Prince; what just and terrible punishment he inflicted on his guilty enemies, and on those who had persisted in their rebellion; and what magnificent rewards and tokens of his royal favor, such as lands, and titles of honor, and priceless treasures, and positions of trust near himself, he ungrudgingly and unsparingly bestowed on his faithful servants. It was delightful to see how the Prince made himself one with them in all their joys, how he consoled them for all the sorrows they had endured for his name's sake, and how he employed them according to the capacity of each in his recovered dominion.

Now was that beautiful island itself again; nay, it recovered more than its former glory, for the Prince made it his especial kingdom. Indeed, his nuptials were celebrated here according to his father's first design. I must not attempt to describe the joy of that lofty bridal. One thing only I record: on that day it was ordered by royal proclamation and blowing of trumpets, that the island should no longer be called *Avehdah*, or "that which is lost," but *Beulah*, which signifies "married," and that the metropolis where he fixed his palace home should henceforth be named *Hephzibah*, that is, "My delight is in her."

WHEN the venerable Oberlin had finished his story, he looked round on the bright eager faces of the children Aimée,

Adolphe and his twin brother Gustave, and the darling Röschen, as if he expected an immediate shower of questions as to the meaning of his parable. Nor would he have had many moments to wait, only Marie, the old nurse, who had been admitted to the little group of listeners at her own earnest request, anticipated all by saying, " May I make so bold, sir, as to ask whether all this really happened or not? For I thought, as you were speaking, my master, be sure, got that from one of the brass bound vellum folios that take up all the lowest shelf of the study bookcase."

" Not quite, good Marie, from either Chrysostom or Augustine," replied Oberlin smiling. " But we will try and make out together by the aid of our Bibles whether something very like this is not happening every day in the history of Christ's church militant here on earth. What, my children, do you understand by the large, beautiful island, Avehdah, or Shulam, as it was first called ? "

"The island," said Aimée, "must mean our world, which God created so pure and lovely that it is said, 'God saw every thing that He had made, and, behold, it was very good.'"[1]

"And the King, then," said Gustave, "must represent God, who owns and governs the world."

"And the Prince," said little Röschen, "is of course the Lord Jesus Christ. I soon saw that."

"And the revolted satrap, Abaddon," added Adolphe, "can only be the devil, who was a murderer from the beginning, and abode not in the truth.[2] I remembered the name, as soon as I heard it, occurring in Revelation. Here it is, 'And they had a king over them, which is the angel of the bottomless pit, whose name in the Hebrew tongue is Abaddon, but in the Greek tongue hath his name Apollyon.'[3] And the meaning is given in the margin, 'that is to say, a destroyer.'"

[1] Gen. i. 31.   [2] John viii. 44.   [3] Rev. ix. 11.

"But before we pass on," inquired Oberlin, "what think you is meant by the easy tribute of fruits and spices and jewels, which the inhabitants rendered to the King, before Abaddon came among them?"

"Are they not," answered Adolphe, after a little pause, "the thoughts and words and acts of loving praise which our Father in heaven requires from all his children?"

"Quite right," replied Oberlin, with a beaming look of approval. "And what can be easier or more delightful for His children to render? Do you remember that even Satan confesses this, in the lines of Milton, which you repeated to me last week?—

> 'Ah, wherefore? He deserved no such return
> From me, whom He created what I was
> In that bright eminence, and with his good
> Upbraided none: nor was His service hard.
> What could be less than to afford Him praise,
> The easiest recompense, and pay Him thanks,
> How due? yet all this good proved ill in me.'

And so, alas, it proved in the poor islanders of Avehdah. What do you understand by

Abaddon, coming over so subtly at first, and stealing the hearts of the people by vessels of curious device and promises of freedom?"

"Why, sir," interposed Marie, "I think I see that now: it was the serpent tempting Adam and Eve with the fruit in the garden, and promising them that they should be as gods if they would only eat it."

"Quite so, Marie," replied Oberlin, "and then you know how when once our first parents gave the devil a foothold in their hearts, the evil spread apace. As men multiplied, sin multiplied. Sin entered into the world and death by sin. The land was as the garden of Eden before them, and behind them a desolate wilderness; until the whole earth, which God created pure, was filled with violence."

"Grandfather," said Aimée, "who are meant by the royal merchants and the King's messengers?"

"Let us take the royal merchants first, my children," answered Oberlin. "Will one of you read Gen. iii. 24; and another Gen. xxviii. 12; and another Matt. xviii. 10; and another Heb. i. 14?"

Aimée reads, "And God placed at the east of the garden of Eden cherubims, and a flaming sword which turned every way, to keep the way of the tree of life."

Adolphe reads, "And Jacob dreamed, and behold a ladder set up on the earth, and the top of it reached to heaven: and behold the angels of God ascending and descending on it."

Röschen reads, "Take heed that ye despise not one of these little ones: for I say unto you, That in heaven their angels do always behold the face of my Father which is in heaven."

Gustave reads, "Are they not all ministering spirits, sent forth to minister to the heirs of salvation?"

"So you see, my children," continued Oberlin, "the Bible tells us of a constant intercourse betwixt heaven and earth from the fall to the present hour, by means of angels. I think, then, that angels may be well signified by the royal merchants."

"And the King's messengers," said Adolphe, "must surely be the prophets and apostles and evangelists, for I have turned to that verse you pointed out to us the other day — 'And the Lord God of their fathers sent to them by His messengers, rising up betimes, and sending; because He had compassion on His people, and on His dwelling-place.'"[1]

"You are right," answered Oberlin, "though the word *angels*, being interpreted, signifies *messengers;* and though these celestial couriers have often brought God's messages to man, as we read both in the Old and the New Testaments, yet our Father generally employs human lips to utter His words. How I long to know, Adolphe, if you will ever be able to use the words yourself, 'We are ambassadors for Christ, as though God did beseech you by us: we pray

[1] 2 Chron. xxxvi. 15.

you in Christ's stead, be ye reconciled to God.'[1] But we must hasten on. What shall we say of those few faithful adherents to the King's cause, whom the messengers sought out in every province of Avehdah?"

"O grandfather," said Gustave, "as you spoke of them, I could not help thinking of the Lord's answer to Elijah, when he complained, 'I, even I, only am left,' and God said to him, 'Yet have I left me seven thousand in Israel, all the knees which have not bowed unto Baal, and every mouth which hath not kissed him.'"[2]

"Yes," continued Aimée, "and did not the time when Abaddon fondly thought he had crushed the witnesses for the truth, mean the long ages between the captivity of Jerusalem and the birth of our Saviour? Oh, I am so often glad that I did not live then. I think they must have been almost the gloomiest times the world ever knew."

"How I wish, grandfather," said Röschen,

[1] 2 Cor. v. 20.   [2] 1 Kings xix. 18.

"you had not passed over that chapter of Avehdah's story which told of the Prince's first visit, when he came without his royal robes or retinue. I thought the little boat was like the manger of Bethlehem. But I shall coax you to read me that chapter one day."

" O Röschen," interrupted Gustave, " you do not understand that all is not written in a parable. Grandfather only meant us to think what would have been in it, if it had been written. I suppose the prison from which the Prince broke loose was the grave from which Jesus rose, and his charge to his servants, before he left them, the last words of the Saviour before He ascended to His Father's right hand."

" Röschen and I," said Oberlin, " will have a talk alone some day about that omitted chapter of the story of Avehdah. But now, what is meant by the checkered success of the long war that followed the Prince's departure ? "

"Is it not," said Aimée, "the history of the last eighteen hundred years — Christianity now apparently conquering whole cities and countries, and now apparently itself conquered and driven from them?"

"It is," replied Oberlin. "What can be more affecting than to think of the once flourishing churches of Jerusalem, and Antioch, and Ephesus, and Corinth, and Carthage, and then to reflect what they are now? But the gates of hell have never prevailed against Christ's holy Church universal, and in every age our dear Master has had His faithful witnesses — sometimes few and feeble — who have borne testimony to the truth, and looked for His promised return. Their hearts have often been faint and weary; but the Church has still held fast to her early creed, 'He shall come again with glory to judge both the quick and the dead, whose kingdom shall have no end.' But what say you to the messenger's visit to the silver mine among the mountains, and gathering a troop of soldiers from those poor enslaved miners on the very eve of the Prince's return?"

"Grandfather," said Adolphe, "is it not what ministers are doing in our own day, when they call men to overcome this present evil world, and fight the good fight of faith?"

"It is, Adolphe, it is," replied Oberlin, with emotion. "For is not the gaining of this world, its pleasures and honors and riches, as the soul's portion, a hard slavery? Men toil early and late, and heap up treasures, but they cannot tell who shall gather them. Then often they fall a-wrangling over the possessions they have so laboriously won. And many are so weary and worn out, they have no heart left to listen to the voice of Jesus. And others, who have gained the world, seem only bent on grasping it tightly and more tightly, as the time draws nearer when they must go and stand before God. I know this has always been so from the beginning, but it seems to me more and more the character of these last days."

"Do you think then, grandfather," asked Aimée, "that these are the very last days, and that the Prince is so very near?"

"Of the day and hour of His return, my child," answered Oberlin, "knoweth no man. But surely there are signs enough to make us think very often and seriously of the words of Jesus, 'When these things begin to come to pass, then look up, and lift up your heads; for your redemption draweth nigh.'[1] The royal herald's trumpet-call in the depth of the cavern, 'The night is far spent, the day is at hand,' has had its counterpart in the wide-spread preaching of the Second Advent of our Lord in these latter times. And I often think we may expect a great ingathering of guests to the King's supper-table from the streets and lanes of the city, and from the highways and hedges of the country, just before the Bridegroom comes, and the door

[1] Luke xxi. 28.

is shut. But what Scriptures do you think bear out the different issues of the herald's invitation?"

"I thought of the prophet's cry, 'Who hath believed our report?'"[1] said Gustave.

"And I, of John Baptist's voice," said Adolphe, "'Prepare ye the way of the Lord.'"[2]

"And I," said Röschen, "of the words of Jesus, in my favorite story of the Ten Virgins — 'At midnight there was a cry made, Behold the Bridegroom cometh, go ye out to meet him.'"[3]

"That does not answer to the hours at all, Röschen," said Gustave. "One was early morning, the other midnight."

"Ah, my children," interposed Oberlin, "the world's midnight may be the Church's morning. But who are signified by those miners who obeyed the messenger and ranged themselves on his side? And what is meant by the white apparel and the

[1] Isa. liii. 1.   [2] Luke iii. 4.   [3] Matt. xxv. 6.

gleaming armor of proof which they put on?"

"Surely, grandfather," said Aimée, "they are all who obey the glad tidings of salvation, and make the promise of their baptism real and true, 'to fight manfully under Christ's banner against sin, the world, and the devil.' And do not the white robes mean the graces of the Holy Spirit? I have never forgotten your telling us of those beautiful garments, mercy, kindness, humility, meekness, long-suffering, all knit together by the golden girdle of love."[1]

"And then," said Gustave, "St. Paul tells us plainly what the armor is, 'Stand, therefore, having your loins girt about with truth, and having on the breastplate of righteousness; and your feet shod with the preparation of the gospel of peace; above all, taking the shield of faith, wherewith ye shall be able to quench all the fiery darts of the wicked; and take the helmet of salvation,

[1] Col. iii. 12-14.

and the sword of the Spirit, which is the the Word of God.'¹ How I wish it was a visible conflict! There would be something so heart-stirring in actually seeing the enemy and grasping the wonderful armor and dealing the blows!"

"It is none the less real, my boy," replied Oberlin, "for being invisible. Perhaps if you had one *sight* of the hosts of darkness, it would be too much for you to bear. Be sure the Captain of our salvation has done wisely in veiling the unseen world till His time is come."

"I suppose," said Adolphe, "the encampment, which the liberated miners joined, points out some beloved church like our own."

"Yes," answered Oberlin, "and here we may safely wait till the Prince returns. Only let us heartily welcome every message which he sends us by his couriers. I think you will recognize the three Advent watchwords,— 'Behold, I come quickly.'² Oh, that our

[1] Ephes. vi. 14–17.   [2] Rev. xxii. 7, 12, 20.

very souls may answer 'Amen: even so, come, Lord Jesus,' for no heart can conceive and no tongue can tell either the misery of His enemies on the one side, or on the other the felicity of His own servants when He sits upon the throne of His glory and says to them, 'Come, ye blessed children of my Father, inherit the kingdom prepared for you from the beginning of the world.' Then will He reward every one according as his work shall be. No act of loyalty and love shall be forgotten. And then shall take place the marriage of the Lamb and the everlasting reunion of heaven and earth. May not the name of that kingdom be well called Beulah, and of its metropolis Hephzibah?"

"OVER THE HILLS HOMEWARD."

THERE was a secluded valley lying some twenty miles inland from the coast of the southern continent in the New World. Betwixt it and the sea was a range of precipitous hills, partly wooded and partly rugged with bluffs of bare granite. The valley itself was fruitful and well watered; though it was liable to the incursions of wild beasts that prowled in the surrounding forests; and, what was a far more serious danger, the region was not seldom exposed to the shocks of severe earthquakes.

It was in this valley that there was the wasted remnant, about thirty in number, of a gallant band of boys and youths who had been induced to leave their native land and settle in this far-away, sequestered spot. It were long to thread all the mazes of their sad story; but the main outlines of it were as follows:—

A crafty and unprincipled colonist obtained a grant of the vale from the semi-barbarous tribes who were the only inhabitants of this zone, in exchange for glass beads and ornaments of trifling value. Having gained their rough signature to a deed of purchase, he left them and sailed away to his mother country, and there described the fertility and resources of the valley in most glowing terms; and by means of his plausible address and forged testimonials he persuaded many parents and guardians, some of them people of substance and of sterling excellence, to commit their children or wards to his care. The ordinary avenues of life were thronged. Some of the lads had failed in passing sundry examinations; and there were many others who had no taste for the quiet occupations of long-established society, in whose hearts the love of enterprise beat quick, and whose friends were not unwilling to pay a substantial premium that the boys should be taught the art of farming in tropical climes, and become themselves in time the proprietors of extensive lands for a mere nominal sum of money.

The issue was that the father and founder, as he called himself, of the proposed colony obtained the charge of nearly one hundred youths, ranging between the ages of fourteen and eighteen; with whom, and in possession of a very considerable capital of ready money, he set sail from their native land. He had consummate address in conversation. The voyage was cheered by his wit and anecdotes and the golden prospects he sketched of certain riches in the country, to which they were bound. The ship was forced by stress of weather to land them in a natural haven far to the north of their proposed point of disembarkation, which, to tell the truth, was very rarely visited by ships, as it lay out of the usual route of mercantile traffic, and the anchorage was exposed and dangerous. The consequence was, that their journey to the valley was long and tedious, encumbered as they were with baggage and provender, and much of it lying through a sandy desert, though they escaped the rugged path over and through the hills.

However, at last their bourn was gained, and for a few weeks all went well. The founder explored with them the marvels and beauties of the valley, and gave them some easy directions as to the cultivation of the plantains and date-palms and vines and other trees of the country. But after a while his instructions became less and less frequent; he was not seen by his pupils for days together; and at last he was nowhere to be found. His tent was empty. His choice portables were all gone. The founder had absconded and left this band of boys and youths to themselves.

Months passed on. For a long while they expected their president would surely return. But he came not. They had no master. Some continued their light labor in the rich, loamy soil. Others idled away their time in useless pastime. Some wandered into the neighboring woods and became the prey it is supposed of lions and leopards, for their companions saw them no more. And now their store of provision was exhausted; and, though the light food of the country supplied many of their necessities, diseases in various forms set in,— fevers and agues and dysentery. This valley, beautiful as it was, proved at certain seasons, from the rankness of its vegetation and the malaria arising from some undrained swamps, most perilous for Europeans. They died off like sheep. All hope of establishing a settlement there was utterly broken up. But how should they return? Weakened and dispirited, they declared that they could not essay the long journey through the desert. The way to the coast over the hills was unknown and beset with dangers — and what should they do if they gained the shore? However, at last a stray native pilgrim, who chanced to pass through the valley, and commiserated their forlorn estate, offered to carry a letter for them to the distant port at which they had landed, whither he himself was bound, and to place it in the hands of the captain of the first vessel which might touch there. This buoyed up their hopes for a while. But as week after week passed by they feared that it was all in vain.

And now all the remaining bonds of discipline were loosed in their little community. The elder youths violently seized that which belonged to the younger. The vicious enticed the weak. There were only three or four among them at most who seemed to remember the lessons of their far-off homes.

One morning, however, when they had given up all hope of receiving any answer to the letter they had entrusted to the pilgrim (the early dews were scarcely dried from the long luxuriant grass), a stranger suddenly appeared among them. His garb was that of a foreigner, but he spoke their language perfectly. He told them that their letter had been faithfully delivered at the distant port, and had fallen into the hands of a captain whose heart was deeply touched by their piteous story; that the captain had diverted his vessel from its ordinary course for their sakes, and that the ship was now lying in the open roadstead on the nearest point of the coast over the hills; that he himself who spoke to them, knowing the country well, had travelled the distance in little more than eight hours, having only set forth long after sunset on the previous evening; but that the captain bade him say he would remain till the same hour on the following morning, so that all might reach the ship. The stranger urged them to set forth without delay; for he said that his own path lay far into the interior of the continent, or he would gladly have returned with them; but that, if they would follow the mountain defile straight towards the sun-rising, they would find at the end of the ravine a narrow track, which though sometimes faintly marked was still sufficient to guide them by aid of a traveller's map, of which he would give a copy to each. It was a map of the pathway across the hills, on which every rock and dell and wood and swamp and bypath was indicated, and the true track was traced in a deep red line all the way. He said that if they set out at once, they might even hope by strenuous effort to reach the coast before or soon after sunset; but that, in case night should overtake them, he would also give to each one who would receive it a traveller's lamp. He showed them how to kindle and feed and trim the lamps, which, he said, small though they were, would by reason of the brightness of the light cast from the silver reflector scare even a wild beast from its attack. And he urged them, if they were in any perplexity, to let the light of the lamp fall upon the map, and they would find their right path marked by arrow-heads all the way to the coast.

I confess I expected that this kind and good man's words would have been greeted with one shout of gratitude from the group of boys, some twenty in number, who listened to him. All had not obeyed the summons to come and hear his message. But I was grievously and bitterly disappointed.

One said that he could not think of leaving behind what remained of his possessions, — they were sorely dwindled as it was, — and how could he carry them over the hills?

Another said they should have had longer warning: how could the captain expect them to start at an hour's notice?

A third said he doubted whether they could do the distance, all over those rugged hills, in twenty-four hours; while a fourth, contradicting his comrade, replied that if the stranger had traversed the route in eight hours, so might they; and that for himself he should wait for the cool of the evening, for he much preferred travelling by night to the glare of a tropical sun.

A fifth answered that he would go so far as to see whether there was such a track at the end of the defile, for he had never observed it, and had grave doubts of its existence.

Another hesitatingly intimated that his decision should depend on that of the rest: he would go if all agreed to go.

While yet another (my heart glowed with indignation as he spoke) asked, with the keen, suspicious air of superior wisdom, how they could be sure they were not being duped and deceived? Very likely the man wanted to lead them into some ambush, and to seize and sell them as slaves.

I expected to see the stranger at once turn away in utter disgust. But no: he drew from the folds of his dress a letter in the captain's handwriting, signed with his name, and sealed with his seal, which verified every word he had uttered. The stranger offered to leave the letter in their hands. He even made excuses for their doubts and suspicions, after the cruel deception they had suffered from the duplicity of the man who had brought them to this valley. He invited explanations. He answered every objection. He again and again urged the need of immediate action. And when most of them still looked upon him with a cold and incredulous gaze, he even entreated them with tears, for he said his heart yearned over their pitiable condition. He then brought out from his traveller's scrip a number of fac-simile maps of the mountain track and several little lamps of beautiful and easy construction, which he took round and offered to one another.

About half the lads accepted the maps,

which they could thrust at once into their bosom; and some five or six of them took the lamps as well. It struck me that more of them wished to do so, but were kept back by false shame, dreading the scorn of one jesting companion, who did not cease from pouring contempt on the stranger's words and turning his gifts into ridicule. However, among those who accepted both map and lamp, I especially marked two boys,—one of whom I will call Fidelis, for his trustful nature was written on his open brow, and the other, Hilaris, for his joyous spirit made him a favorite with all. Fidelis also, I saw, craved a map and lamp for a bosom friend of his, named Urban, who from indolence had not risen from his couch that morning to listen to the stranger's words. These were freely given; and a small supply was left for any boys who might be afterwards disposed to make use of them. And so the stranger passed on his way, not without many an earnest word of advice to Fidelis and Hilaris and the others who had taken the maps and lamps; and not without many a sorrowful and compassionate look on those who had refused them.

When he was gone, Fidelis at once sought out his friend Urban, and told him all the stranger had said, and pleaded his cause so successfully that Urban thanked him with tears in his eyes, sprang from his couch, and hastily dressing himself thrust the map and lamp into the folds of his garment; and together they joined the large group of lads, amid which Hilaris was standing and talking full of a joyous hope of seeing his fatherland once more. His bright words had evidently quickened the hopes of many.

However, one boy would stay to change his attire, another to mend his sandals, another to find a jewelled ring which he had lost; while another insisted, and with more show of reason, that they should at least partake of one hearty meal before their long journey. Hilaris in vain reminded them that the stranger said the track, along which they were to travel, had supplied him and would supply them with all the food they would require for their one day's journey, and that they might fearlessly drink of the crystal streams which would cross their path. But this and other like questions were so long debated, that Fidelis looking up saw to his dismay that the sun was already past midday.

Then he and Hilaris frankly said they would not stay one minute more; those might join them who liked; but that for themselves they were resolved to set out then and there. Urban at once started up, and two or three more, and they set forth, though some implored them to tarry if only half an hour more, and others pointed the finger of scorn at them, and others hurled stones in derision after them.

The three friends, Fidelis, Hilaris, and Urban, pressed on in front; for they agreed that so many precious hours had been lost they must now redouble their efforts. But as they walked on they exchanged many pleasant thoughts of the stranger's kindness, and of the captain's disinterested goodness, and of the delight it would be to be on board a homeward-bound vessel, and above all to tread the shore of their beloved country. Engrossed with this converse, they had almost forgotten the comrades who set out with them, till looking back they saw them loitering by a flowery bank, npon which one had thrown himself at full length. They shouted to them aloud to come on, but the sultry air only brought the answer, "There is no need for haste, tarry awhile, we are weary." So the three pressed on alone, and at length made their way to the end of the defile. There looking carefully among the bushes they found the narrow foot-track of which the stranger had told them; and having certified themselves by the map that it was the right path, they pushed on bravely and cheerily, and climbed the glen by the side of the torrent.

How glad they were then that they had not put off their journey till nightfall; for the track, though it always revealed itself to a careful search, and could then be identified with the red arrow-pointed line traced in their chart, was often difficult to distinguish at first from other paths by which it was intersected.

When they emerged from the brushwood at the head of the glen, they came to an open moorland stretching in far ranges upward; and here they were even more thankful for their maps, for the waters from the hills had settled in the hollows and turned many a spot, which looked from a distance like a beautiful greensward, into a dangerous quagmire. Their pathway often wound round the edge of a treacherous morass; or they had to spring from one rocky stepping-stone to another, through swamps on either side all overgrown by moss and luxuriant rushes. But though they occasionally slipped, and more than once had to retrace their steps when they thought they had discovered a short cut to a distant point and found to their cost that way was impassable, — yet they never consulted their maps in vain; and at length the moors were safely passed, and they trod with more confidence the elastic heather which clothed the ridges of the upper table-land.

Fidelis, however, often had to point out to Urban, who was disposed to lag behind, how fast the sun was sloping toward the west, and how the purple clouds told that they should have to finish their journey under the wing of night. Thus spurring each other to fresh efforts, they pressed on the more eagerly, and by dint of arduous walking and climbing they reached the crest of the range of hills just as the sun was sinking in the western horizon. Its last rays fell upon the blue, far-off ocean. The boys shouted, " The sea, the sea ! " and leaped for joy. Here they found a spring of delicious water, and freely partook of the last grapes and maize-corn they had plucked in passing down the valley. They

looked back on the way they had trodden with much thankfulness and forward with hopefulness, though Hilaris confessed himself much disappointed at not seeing the sails or even mast-head of the vessel on the distant sparkling sea. Fidelis answered it was doubtless moored beneath the lofty cliffs, and that they could not expect to see it till they neared the shore.

But now — for twilight is very short in the tropics — the darkness soon came down upon them. So they lit their lamps, and kept carefully along the narrow track, Hilaris first, then Urban, and Fidelis bringing up the rear. But on that high table-land there were no mists. The air was life. The cool of night was most invigorating after that long, sultry afternoon. And the burning stars above them, among which Fidelis pointed out with deep joy the Southern Cross, seemed like angel friends now the sun was gone.

So they walked on in good cheer, till they

came to a sudden dip in the hillside, where was a deep glen forming a little ravine by itself. This glen was filled with a white, silvery mist, that clung around the rocks and furze-bushes. It was an exhalation from a neighboring marsh, but was as impenetrable as a fog-bank. They could not see three feet before them. Here they were in doubt. Urban strongly advised that they should descend the hill on the grassy ridge which hemmed in the glen on every side. But to this Fidelis would by no means consent; for on consulting their maps they all agreed that the red arrow-pointed line lay through, not round it. So they began to feel their way; but, oh! this was weary work. Now they had to hold the lamp close to the map, and now quite low to their feet, to be sure that they were in the right track. Again and again Urban would have had them turn aside, but the hopefulness of Hilaris and the trust of Fidelis held on and held out. More than once they thought they heard the roar of wild beasts, though apparently not very near them; and shortly after the very ground beneath their feet seemed to shake as with the tremor of an earthquake. Several times they were compelled to stop from sheer exhaustion; for you must be aware that it was a very different thing breathing that thick oppressive mist from imbibing the free mountain air. Their lungs seemed cloyed, and their heart heaved wearily. Fidelis said that he thought they must have been more than two hours threading their way through that glen, and bitterly lamented the time they had lost on the previous forenoon. Had they started at once, as the stranger urged them, they would have escaped this marsh fog. However, their only comfort was, the map said they were in the right track.

And so it proved. At last they arrived at the lower edge of the glen, and the mist became thinner, and the outline of the rocks clearer, and the furze-bushes and the trunks of trees more discernible; and soon the beautiful stars again gladdened their eyes.

The trees of which I spoke, though few and sparse at first, became thicker and closer continually, until it was evident that their onward path lay through the dense forest. The track now was narrower and more overgrown with brambles than ever, and in the dim light their hands and faces were often torn with the entangling briars. As thus they painfully struggled on, Fidelis, who was behind, heard the stealthy tread of some beast of prey. He told Urban, and Urban Hilaris. Their hearts beat quick; but standing closely together they held their bright lamps aloft. It was enough; with a low growl the lion (for such it was) slunk into the thick bushes, and molested them no more. The thought, however, of this ravenous beast being so near them made them forget their weariness and the sharpness of the thorns. They pressed on with redoubled speed, until they left the forest behind them and stood at the base of a rugged ascent.

And here a greater sorrow befell Fidelis

"OVER THE HILLS HOMEWARD." 95

and Hilaris than any they had yet experienced. Urban, who had kept with them so long, refused to accompany them any further. And this was the reason. He had seen from the sunset ridge the line of the country sloping toward the sea, and had counted on a gradual descent from that vantage-ground. And now, when travel-worn and foot-sore, after passing through the foggy ravine and the briary forest, he found the track again climbing one of the lesser hills which he had overlooked from the summit, instead of winding along its base, he was altogether discouraged and chagrined. He was sure the track would deceive them. He was certain the map was wrong. Why should they not turn to the right, and then keep straight down toward the sea? They could not be very far off now from the coast. Had they not walked on and on for twelve hours? Fidelis and Hilaris might climb the steep without him. But as for himself, now that they had gained the open, where there were no mists, and where the beasts of prey came not, he should rest where he was for awhile, and then strike downward in the direction he pointed to the sea-shore.

It was in vain that Fidelis argued with him, and Hilaris sought to cheer him. They even took him by either arm and began to drag him up the slope. All was of no use; Urban was doggedly resolute. Perhaps they wasted an hour in persuasion, and then Fidelis sorrowfully said to Hilaris:—
"Brother, we must go on; we shall only die with him here, and if we reach the ship we may induce the captain to stay a few hours for him." Their hearts were torn with anguish. But what could they do more? Twice they returned several hundred yards down the steep to entreat him. But Urban threw himself on the ground, and bade them leave him to himself.

So the two friends finally addressed themselves to the remainder of their journey. Their hearts were knit more closely than ever together; and many were the earnest prayers they prayed for their companion. Yet their own path had its toils and intricacies, its doubts, and difficulties, and dangers; up one steep and down the next, climbing many a slippery rock, and footing wearily the stony path with here and there a beautiful meadow of tender grass as they drew nearer and nearer the coast. Here also vines bent over them, of which they plucked the refreshing clusters of grapes, until at last Hilaris said to his brother: "Surely the eastern sky is tinged with streaks of pearl;" and a few minutes afterwards, "See that ruby glow;" and a few minutes later, "See that golden belt of cloud;" and a few minutes more, "Oh, joy! here is the first beam of the morning sun."

That very moment they came from behind a natural wall of cliff along which the track had wound, and stood upon the bold headland. And there, a few hundred feet below them, lay the gallant vessel. The boys shouted and threw their caps into the air for joy. The signal was seen by the look-out man at the foremast, and their feeble shout was answered by a hearty cheer from the ship. A boat's crew put off. The boys rapidly descended a rough gully worn by a winter torrent, hurried as fast as they might over the shingly beach, sprang into the boat, and in less than half an hour stepped on board that noble ship, called "Salvator," whose sign was an anchor biting the rock.

It was some time before they could speak. But when somewhat revived with food, they told their story to the captain, while the officers and crew clustered round, Hilaris taking up the tale when Fidelis broke down. They both wept when they spoke of Urban. The kind-hearted captain, though he said the mercury was falling in his weather-glass, and he dared not remain on that exposed coast twelve hours more, and, indeed, himself had little hope of the boy's finding his way, promised to delay sailing till noon. Hour after hour passed by.. The twelve o'clock bells were struck. And then the captain bid the sailors weigh anchor; and the foresail was set, and the ship swung round; when suddenly Fidelis, who had kept his eye ranging the shore, shouted, "There he is; yes, there is Urban." And he it was indeed, bemired, and bruised, and bleeding, his clothes torn to shreds — yet Urban himself. Seeing the vessel set sail, he recklessly dashed into the sea, as he was, and swam out into the waves. Again the boat was lowered, and willing hearts and arms pulled towards the lad, as he wildly buffeted the billows. And well it was they rowed so hard; for not only was his strength failing, but just as they dragged him into the boat a shark turned on its side and opened its ravenous jaws to devour him. A few seconds more, and he would have been the prey of the sea-monster. So nearly was Urban lost.

I must not attempt to tell at length the

tale of his sufferings and hair-breadth escapes, as he told it to Fidelis and Hilaris that day: the sense of utter desolation he experienced, when he found they had indeed gone on their way: the hour of unrest as he lay upon the heather, for he heard more than once the roar of lions in the skirts of the forest through which they had passed, and was afraid to close his wearied eyelids even for a moment: the vexation with which at last he sprang up and hurried along the level moor till he came to broken ground and sharp declivities again: the utter perplexity he felt when he found his progress stopped by an impetuous torrent which had worn a deep channel among the slippery precipitous rocks: the despair with which he remembered his chart was utterly useless now, and his lamp of very little avail without the map: the trouble with which he made his way along the side of the torrent, often falling heavily and bruising himself severely in the darkness: the tearing of his clothes every step by cactuses and other prickly shrubs which baffled him on every side: how his face, his hands, his arms, his legs were lacerated with thorns: how once, springing from a thicket upon what he thought was an open plot of grass, he sank into a deep quag almost up to his armpits, and, hardly grasping a furze-bough, struggled out, but not without the loss of both his shoes in the slough, and the quenching of the lamp which he still held in the other hand: how then he thought he should have laid him down and died, if he had not caught a glimpse of the Southern Cross to which Fidelis had directed them at the beginning of the night: how this had encouraged him to struggle on with bleeding feet hour after hour, now floundering through swamps, now on firmer ground, and now again through glens perplexed with briars and thorns: how at last the morn began to break, but his heart sank within him as he thought it would be the signal for the ship setting sail: how still he toiled on, and as the day dawned was astonished and grieved beyond measure to find himself, after all his efforts, not far from the spot where he had parted from his friends. But could he be wrong? There was the long range of hills which they had descended together; there was the forest; there was the steep they had climbed, not so very high or hard after all in the daylight. And then he told with what trembling anxiety he felt in the folds of his tattered dress for his long-forgotten map. Yes, there it was, wet and stained, but safe. And now an eager search discovered the track. His tears fell fast upon it, for he feared it was too late. Still it was his only chance. Snatching a few berries as he passed to stay his hunger, and scooping in his hands the water from a wayside burn, he allayed his craving hunger and thirst, and hurried on as fast as his poor naked feet would suffer him. Many were the groans the sharp rocks cost him. But he never took his eye from the track, save to look upon his now doubly precious chart and certify himself that he was right. Oh, the intense relief when he passed from the stony wold to a beautiful meadow, and when without slackening his pace he could pluck the grapes which festooned the trees above him! Still often a few hundred yards of turf would be succeeded by rocky climbing again. The sun now beat upon his head. But at last he, like his friends, passed from under the shelter of the granite bluff, and stood, almost unawares, upon the edge of the cliff. He said he wellnigh fainted with joy when he saw the vessel still moored below the cliff: but listening intently he heard the measured song of the sailors as they heaved the anchor, and his heart leaped into his mouth as the canvas was sheeted home and the vessel began to move. He sprang from rock to rock down the channel which the torrent had worn in the cliff, and, throwing up his arms wildly into the air, dashed into the waves.

Fidelis and Hilaris knew the rest. They could only grasp his hands for joy, and the three lads knelt down together on the deck and thanked God for his escape.

But I must not stay to tell all the kindness of the captain and the crew, and all the comfort of their rapid voyage home, and all the sorrowful memories of the valley and those left behind, and all the joy with which they sighted the shores of their native land, and all the hearty welcome of beloved ones there, and how they found the hymn which they often sang together delightfully verified:—

> " Why these fears ? behold, 'tis Jesus
>   Holds the helm and guides the ship.
> Spread the sails and catch the breezes
>   Sent to waft us through the deep
> To the regions where the mourners **cease to weep.**

> " O what pleasures there await us ;
>   There the tempests cease to **roar;**
> There it is that those who hate us
>   Can molest our peace no more :
> Trouble ceases on that tranquil, **happy shore.**"

WHEN Oberlin stopped there was a pause of some minutes. The hearts of his grandchildren were touched with the story, and their eyes were full of tears. But when at last the old man broke the silence by saying that his parable had taken him so long to read they had but a short time to discuss it, Adolphe hesitatingly replied, "Grandfather, I think I saw the meaning of the night journey over the hills; but I could not at all make out what the fraud of that bad man, who drew the boys from their native land to that far-off valley and then went off with the money given him, signified."

"A parable, Gustave," said Oberlin, "seldom stands on four legs. See that solid globe of glass upon yonder polished rosewood table. It rests upon one point not larger than the point of a needle, and yet all its weight presses on the table. So, often many things in a parable go to make up the picture; and it is the central thought of the picture which speaks to our hearts. But, do you know, something very like that bad man's conduct really happened a few years ago, and many young friends of mine were actually enticed away by him. However, it will be enough for us to think to-night of the meaning of the latter part of my story, only reminding ourselves that the world is something like that beautiful sequestered valley, with its rich fruitful soil, but with wild beasts of prey, such as sin and Satan, ranging near, and exposed to sudden earthquakes which may wrap all in ruin; that they who will have their portion in this life are, like those young colonists, doomed to certain disappointment; that the god of this world, who promises them all kinds of pleasure and profit in his service here, will never redeem his pledges; that blight, like the malaria fevers of that valley, will sooner or later fall on the fondest hopes of those who set their affections here; and that the voice is heard in the hearts of the children of wisdom, 'Arise ye, and depart; for this is not your rest: because it is polluted, it shall destroy you, even with a sore destruction.'[1] This is our pilgrim call."

"Then, grandfather," said Aimée, "was not the messenger like Evangelist in 'Pilgrim's Progress,' who pointed Christian to the wicket gate?"

"Yes," answered Oberlin, "my parable might be called a short 'Pilgrim's Progress,' compressed into one day's journey; and I often, when making it, thought of the text, 'Give glory to the Lord your God, before He cause darkness, and before your feet stumble upon the dark mountains, and, while ye look for light, He turn it into the shadow of death, and make it gross darkness.'"[2]

"O I did so wish," said little Röschen, "that all the boys had started at once, when the stranger entreated them to go, and offered them maps and all they wanted. It was so foolish of them not to go. He said

---

[1] Micah ii. 10.   [2] Jer. xiii. 16.

they might have even reached the ship before nightfall."

"God grant," said Oberlin, "that all my children may start for home in the early dewy morning;" and the old man leaned his head on his clasped hands for a few moments in solemn prayer; and then looking round his circle asked, "Can you explain from your Bibles the excuses they made?"

"Was not the lad who would carry his possessions with him," said Gustave, "like the young man who came running to Jesus,[1] but would not sell all that he had and follow Him?"

"And," said Aimée, "was not the one who replied they could not be expected to start at an hour's notice like Felix, who answered Paul, 'Go thy way for this time; when I have a convenient season, I will call for thee?'"[2]

"Now I thought," interrupted Gustave, "the one who would wait for the cool of the

[1] Mark x. 17.   [2] Acts xxiv. 25.

evening was like Felix, and the boy who said he would go so far as to look for the track at the end of the defile like Agrippa when he answered Paul, 'Almost thou persuadest me to be a Christian.'[1] What cowards those were who waited to see what the others would do!"

"And yet," replied Oberlin, "it requires no small courage and no little faith to do what Lot did, when he forsook Sodom, though his alarm seemed mockery to his sons-in-law. And there are many would-be wise men, and many doubters, and many infidels, who will throw scorn on the warnings of the Gospel. But I see you quite understand the key to this part of my parable, and we must speak for a few minutes of those who obeyed the stranger's invitation."

"Why, grandfather," said Adolphe, "*Fidelis* I know means 'faithful,' and *Hilaris* 'joyful,' for I had them both in my Latin exercise last week. What does *Urban* mean?"

[1] Acts xxvi. 28.

"Polished and refined," answered Oberlin, "like one who dwells in a city (*urbs*), and knows all the courtesies of society. Perhaps to live the pilgrim's life and to march over the hills homeward is the harder for such an one than for those who move in a lower walk of life; for we read, 'God has chosen the poor of this world, rich in faith, and heirs of the kingdom which He hath promised to them that love Him.'[1] What do you understand by the map and lamp, Marie?"

"Well, sir," answered the old nurse humbly, "I thought the map surely meant the Bible; but I do not know what the lamp can be."

"I thought at first," said Aimée, "that the lamp was the light of the Holy Spirit — but then they did not want it when the sun shone, and we want the teaching of the Holy Spirit at all times."

"May not light in itself, whether the light of the sun by day or of the lamp by night,"

[1] James ii. 5.

asked Oberlin, " well signify the teaching of the blessed Spirit who teaches us by His own written word? What was the prayer one of you repeated to me this morning about light?"

" That was my verse," little Röschen said: " ' O send out Thy light and Thy truth: let them lead me; let them bring me unto Thy holy hill, and to Thy tabernacles.'[1] I did not think it would come into our parable this evening."

" And yet," said her grandfather, " in that verse you have both the chart and the light we need to shine upon the chart beautifully expressed. And just as those young travellers found the map of no use without the light, and the light of little use without the map, so the Bible is of no use to us without the teaching of the Holy Spirit; and generally the Holy Spirit, who has given the Bible to be our guide, does not lead us many steps without it. But we must hasten on."

[1] Psalm xliii. 3.

"Was not the glimpse of the sea, which they got from the crest of the hills," asked Aimée, " a prospect of the rest which remaineth for the people of God?[1] And yet they did not see the ship. Does this mean, we do not see the angels who are to carry us to glory till we get to the very end of life?"

"And did not the foggy glen mean a time of trial and darkness, like that David passed through when he said, ' Yea, though I walk through the valley of the shadow of death, I will fear no evil: for Thou art with me'?"[2] asked Adolphe.

"And I suppose, then," said Gustave, "the tangled forest means the world with its pleasures and cares, and the growl of the lion the wrath of the devil."

"When the lion slunk away," said Röschen, "I thought of the text, ' Resist the devil, and he will flee from you.'[3] But why, oh! why, grandfather, did Urban forsake them when he had come so far?"

[1] Heb. iv. 9.   [2] Psalm xxiii. 4.   [3] James iv. 7.

"Do we not read of many pilgrims, my child," answered Oberlin, "who walk steadily on for a while, and then have sad grievous backslidings or falls, from which they suffer all their after-life? Such was Jacob, and such was David; though these saints had a brighter after-path than poor Urban's was."

"Does Urban's lamp being quenched in the swamp mean that the Holy Spirit ever quite refuses to show those who forsake the narrow path what is their duty?" asked Adolphe.

"I think it may set forth," answered Oberlin, "that they sometimes quite lose the *comfort* of His help and the *joy* of His salvation.[1] God's own faithful servants, too, sometimes walk in darkness and have no light.[2] But Urban, you remember, after a while caught a glimpse of the Southern Cross, which may well tell under another figure of the Holy Spirit pointing the sinner's eye to Jesus and Him crucified. But our time is gone. We may speak to-morrow of many other lessons

[1] Psalm li. 12.   [2] Isa. l. 10.

which this parable suggests. Only now remember that the three boys, though Urban's lot was very different from that of Fidelis and Hilaris, pressed on till they reached the shore and the ship, and so were safely borne over the waters to their distant fatherland. God grant that not one of us may fail of reaching that better heavenly country, — that region where the mourners cease to weep!"

THE PLAGUE-STRICKEN CITY.

HERE was a gloom in the marble city, the city of palaces, Genoa la Superba. The dreaded plague, which appeared first in the kingdom of Kathay, had gradually proceeded westward to Constantinople and Egypt: thence it had passed into Greece, and, creeping along the shores of the Mediterranean, had at length, in the autumn of A.D. 1348, enveloped in its disastrous embrace the sunny clime of Italy. In Florence the people were dying by thousands; and it is credibly reported, that in that beautiful city and its immediate environs sixty thousand persons fell victims to this scourge of God. Genoa, favored by the freshness of prevailing winds from the north-west and by the salubrity of its encircling hills, was spared to the last. But when the wind veered round to the south and east, and then died away to a mere breath, it was far different. The sultry air had never been known to be so oppressive. A heavy cloud rested over the city by day and night, obscuring the sunshine and blotting out the stars. A boding dread seemed to overshadow all hearts. And this was quickened into lively alarm when one morning it was rumored that several cases of the fatal distemper had certainly appeared in the Lazaretto.

The Genoese, however, that day tried to console themselves by the thought that the sufferers in that hospice were of the lowest order, and already enfeebled by disease. Their comfort was brief-lived. The next night physicians were hastily summoned not only to the lowly tenements of artisans, but to palaces of the nobles, and mansions of the wealthy merchants in every part of the city. The old streets of Genoa, as you know, are built so closely together to shut out the burning rays of the summer sun, that you might almost shake hands with your opposite neighbor from the upper stories across the narrow causeways. It was a strange, unwonted sight to see messengers making their way by torchlight through the intricate passages, not with instruments of music and gaily attired guests, but in silence and haste seeking out those who professed any knowledge of medicine. And all the next day the cases multiplied with fearful rapidity; and on the third night the physicians, worn out with fatigue, were far too few for those who imploringly demanded their aid.

Now was heard the sharp cry or the low groan of pain. The heavy air seemed to sigh and sob with the grief of mourners. And the frequent tolling of the great bell in the Campanile added to the general consternation. To allay this cause of alarm, a council was hastily summoned very early in the morning, and a decree made that no passing-bell for the dying or the dead should be rung within the city walls. Also, to prevent contagion, it was enacted that on the door of each house containing infected persons or corpses a black cross should be painted, and a black flag hung across the head of those streets which were most severely visited with the plague. But, alas! it was soon found that the pestilence which walketh in darkness had spread in that one night to almost every quarter of the city.

As the hours wore on, all faces gathered blackness and all hearts meditated terror. The symptoms of this awful malady greatly varied with the different constitutions of those it attacked. In some cases all the agony was in the throat; and the very channel of the breath of life was choked with putrefying sores in the course of three or four hours: the unhappy patient died of suffocation. In other cases a strange dizziness seized the brain: the man was struck to the earth when sitting in his house or walking in the street; and though there were few signs of suffering, these instances were generally fatal in less than twelve hours. In many more cases the first indication was the breaking out of burning spots, which in an incredibly short space of time became ulcerous sores on the chest or arms or other parts of the body; while in not a few instances it appeared that, without any visible sign except a hectic flush in the cheek and a strange lustre in the eye, the disease attacked the region of the heart in all its virulence. The corpses of those who died thus turned black very shortly after death. But with one and all the stroke of pestilence seemed accompanied with an insatiable thirst. Water was eagerly swallowed, but it did not seem to slake the raging fever within. Some thought that the wells of the city must themselves be poisoned by the subtle infection of the plague. Others thought that the meat was the source of danger; and indeed much cattle died; so they abstained from all animal food. But, do what men might, death met them at every turn. And when once stricken, despair was written in the face of every sufferer.

Hour by hour the deaths multiplied. No one put on mourning apparel for the nearest relatives. Funerals ceased. Few could bury their own dead. But at intervals of six hours what was called "the dead cart" passed through the streets: a hand-bell was rung; and the driver, as he came near any house with the cross upon it, cried aloud, "Bring out your dead." To this call the answer of the inmates was often a wail of sorrow as they brought their dead to the door, for the most part only wrapped in the winding-sheet of the couch where they had breathed their last. The bodies, thus borne away on this general bier, were thrown indiscriminately into deep trenches which were dug on the inner side of the quay.

Genoa had been noted for the vivacity of its society, and for the strength of those ties which bind kindred and neighbors together. But the plague had not brooded one short week over the city before this sympathy of hearts seemed to have almost disappeared. There were some noble exceptions. But for the most part, under the icy touch of a hopeless despondency, parents looked coldly and gloomily on their stricken children, and children on their stricken parents. Neighbors shrank from neighbors, and friends deserted friends. The physicians in many instances themselves succumbed to the pestilence; and oftentimes it was only by the offer of very large rewards they could be persuaded to attend at some rich man's bedside. Nor is this to be marvelled at; for, when they came, their drugs were almost powerless and their skill unavailing.

Many more of the inhabitants would fain have escaped on board the galleys and merchant vessels, with which a few days before the noble harbor had been crowded. But these had most of them slipped their cables the second night and put out to sea; and of the few terror-stricken fugitives who reached their decks, several had the seeds in them of the dreadful plague, and so infected the crews that the ships were left absolutely without any hands to work them, and drifted helplessly over the waters without captain or helmsman, or any to set or reef the sails.

The hills, however, surrounding the town on every side but the harbor, afforded some a more accessible shelter. They were dotted with rudely constructed huts, in which hundreds of survivors, leaving sick friends behind them, sought to escape the malaria of the city. But the hill-sides proved no secure asylum: the pestilence followed them there. Yet their flight added to the strange solitude

THE PLAGUE-STRICKEN CITY. 123

of the streets; and the ninth day of the plague in Genoa realized the eloquent words of Tacitus, *Dies modo per silentium vastus, modo ploratibus inquies.*[1]

It was at this time of Genoa's sorest need that a stranger, clad in mean attire, rowed in a little boat into the harbor. The ship, on board of which he came, hove to three or four miles off shore, dropped this tiny craft astern, and then sailing away was seen no more.

The stranger's name was Fra Benedict. He seemed scarcely fifty years of age; but his benevolent brow was worn with deep lines of thought and care. To one who questioned whence he came, he simply answered, "From the sunrising:" to another who demanded how he ventured to set foot on their infected shore, he replied, "For love:" and to a third who asked him whether, if he survived the plague, he intended to settle in Genoa, he

---

[1] "A day now desolate in its silence, and now perplexed with lamentations."

said, with a sweet and tender smile, "No, brother: I am going home." But in truth he came so quietly and unobtrusively, and men's hearts were so preoccupied by their terrible calamities, that few, except those who were listlessly standing on the water's edge, concerned themselves about the landing of this solitary stranger in their harbor. Yet had they known all he was and all the help he could minister to the sick and dying, I think the whole city would have flocked to the marble pier to welcome him.

One breath may speak volumes. Fra Benedict had discovered a sovereign remedy for the plague! He made no secret of the healing virtue of the drug he used. It was an inexpensive simple, but needed skilful and careful application; and then no case had been found too hard for its wonderful properties. When administered in the earliest stage of the disease, its effects were generally marked and often immediate. And, even when the distemper had taken deeper root, by patient and persevering endeavors the sufferer usually recovered after a few days. It was only in a very few and rare instances, and these generally far advanced towards the fatal end, when the sick man desperately refused to comply with his directions, that the malignity of the disease seemed to baffle the art of the physician.

As he said, he came from the East; and he had tracked this terrible plague from land to land and city to city. It were long to tell all the privations and perils he had endured in ministering to those stricken down by it. And probably fame would have heralded his glory far and wide, but for one thing, which generally in every place set the great and learned against him: he always refused payment. Indeed his only condition of attendance was that men should receive his services freely and without price; for he said the work was wages and the hue of returning health in the sick man's face his reward. So his ministry had always chiefly lain among the poor.

So it was in Genoa. On landing at the quay, Fra Benedict at once made his way to the lowest part of the city where the plague was raging most violently. This gave great offence to a few wealthy traders who heard of it, and who affirmed the man's credentials probably would not bear investigation, or he would no doubt have first inquired for the College of Physicians, who were consulting that day for many hours on the best steps to retard the progress of the pestilence. Benedict chose his lodging in what was known as a " plague house ;" for it was set apart as a hospital to which the poor, if they were so minded, might bring their stricken friends. From thence he sent forth messages and letters of invitation, simply stating the fact that he had found a certain cure for the pestilence, and entreating all sufferers to send for him without delay. And forthwith he began his work, and treated many cases among the poor with marvellous success.

Perhaps more would have applied to him; but just at that time the priests affirmed that one of their number had been favored with a miraculous vision, revealing to him that if the Genoese would build a chapel or hermitage in honor of a nun who had died a few years before, the plague would begin to subside; and that those who contributed to its erection would be cured if ill, and protected if whole. It was perfectly marvellous how this fiction obtained credit with the people. But so it was; the nobles showered jewels and gems of priceless value, and the traffickers gold and silver, and even the poorest would bring their last copper coins to cast into the votive treasury. Nay, the chief men and women of the city vied with each other who should have the honor of carrying the stones and timber and mortar to the hermitage, which was being built on a gentle slope without the city walls.

To give one instance, out of many, of the way in which this foolish superstition thwarted

Fra Benedict's ministry of mercy. The third day after his arrival he had been summoned hastily to the glorious palace of Leonardi, whom report said to be the richest merchant prince of Genoa, but who now lay among his crimson silk shuddering with the first chills of the pestilence. Benedict was ascending the marble staircase, when he was met by a procession of several priests and servants, with bags of gold and caskets of jewels, which they were carrying to the site of the hermitage. He with difficulty made his way through the throng, and when he came to the sick man's chamber door, was refused admittance. Leonardi was so satisfied with the immense sums he had given, far exceeding any offerings the saint had received elsewhere, that he believed the assurance of a priest who persuaded him that a tribute of such fabulous wealth would certainly purchase his recovery, and that now to submit to the treatment of a poor vagrant physician would offend the saintly patron whose aid he

was invoking. So Fra Benedict was courteously but firmly urged to depart.

As he was sadly leaving the beautiful portico, where the cool fountain, scattering spray on the orange blossoms, seemed almost a mockery of this death-shadowed home, Benedict observed the runner, who had fetched him hither so hastily, lying at the foot of a marble column. His countenance was ashy pale. Going up to him, Benedict took him kindly by the hand and said, " My friend, the plague is awork in your veins : suffer me to help you." The man demurred for a while, saying he had cast his mite into the coffer of the procession as they swept by, and he thought all would be well. But as the good physician reasoned with him, a sharp spasm of pain convulsed his frame, and he murmured, " Do what you can for me." Benedict, having ministered his remedy to him, left him in the charge of an attached fellow-servant ; and, returning a few hours after, found him already convalescent. But a loud wailing from the upper story told that the master had died, just as the procession re-entered the house, having deposited their offerings at the shrine of the saint.

The record of Fra Benedict's experiences that morning may serve as an example of the treatment he generally met with among the rich and great men of the world. Shortly after he left Leonardi's palace, he passed the stately porch of Rinaldo, the treasurer of the city. Rinaldo himself was there, gazing anxiously down the street, apparently looking for some persons who came not. Seeing Benedict pass, Rinaldo called to him, and begged him if he met a group of servants whom he had sent to summon Lorenzo de' Medici, a learned and celebrated leech, to his wife, to hasten their steps, as she was in great agony, and he did not like to leave her. Benedict entreated that he might be allowed himself to minister to her. But the treasurer replied by asking hurriedly what the nature of his treatment might be, and what his charge for administering it. And when the other answered that it was a very inexpensive drug, and that his attendance was free to all without money, Rinaldo almost rudely implored him to go on his way, assuring him he had discovered long ago that gratuitous remedies were worthless. He would not be reasoned with.

So Fra Benedict passed on, and scarcely half a mile from Rinaldo's house met the servants, carrying the empty palanquin in which Lorenzo de' Medici was to have been borne by them. Giving them their master's message, he asked where Lorenzo might be. They shook their heads and answered, "He is himself sick of the plague." This was enough to attract Benedict: he made his way to the great physician's house, and asked permission to see him. This was courteously accorded him. But the dying man firmly refused his offers of help, saying that he had himself lost faith in all means of cure, but was certain that if any could avail, the potent drug he had just swallowed would carry him through the crisis of this attack. Alas, it proved a mere palliative. Lorenzo de' Medici died that night.

But from Lorenzo's lips Benedict heard that the noted philosopher and naturalist, Giovanni, whose house joined to his own, was likewise stricken down with the plague. As his custom was, Fra Benedict went immediately and offered his remedy; but he was doomed again to meet with repulse. For the philosopher having demanded to see the recipe of his cure, at once pronounced that it was far too simple to touch so terrible a disease, adding that he had the utmost confidence in an elaborate concoction of his own devising, which was distilled from more than fifty herbs and aromatic spices.

A shade of mournful pity, not unmingled with disappointment, saddened the countenance of Benedict as he left the wealthy quarter of the city and made his way to his lodgings through the squalid dwellings of the poor. As he was passing down a very narrow thoroughfare, in former days thronged, but now almost deserted, he heard the signal-bell of the dead cart: it paused before a house that was tenanted in apartments by artisans, and two shrouded forms were cast in. When the cart passed on, Benedict lingered at the threshold, and thinking that he caught the faint echo of a child's groan, he went in. There he saw, in a large but scantily furnished room, three children, all stricken with the same pestilence, of which their father and mother had died a few hours before. They were the bodies of their parents which had just been borne from the door. The names of the three children were Claude, Guido, and Beatrice. It was the wailing cry of little Beatrice, her mother's darling, which had fallen on Benedict's ear, and arrested his onward footstep.

The three children, though all ill, were suffering in different ways. Claude, who had been attacked first, was frequently convulsed with sharp spasms of pain, and then his eyes seemed as if they would start from their sockets; and when the paroxysm was over he would lie for a few minutes as if he were dead, only to be roused by a new agony. Benedict drew near and spoke to him in the gentlest voice; but the poor boy turned away his face in utter hopelessness, saying, "For me you can do nothing, nothing, nothing: see if you can aid poor Guido or little Beatrice."

Benedict turned and looked on Guido, but he shook his head doubtfully. The lad seemed overpowered with a heavy slumber. There was a terrible numbness about his heart, and a cold stare in his eye. Once Benedict roused him and put the healing medicine to his lips. Oh, had he swallowed it, all might yet have been well! But with a sudden and strange energy he cried out aloud, "It is too late: too late!" and thrust away the ministering hand, and clenching his teeth firmly, sank down into a state of apparent unconsciousness.

The kind-hearted physician turned to Beatrice, — the quicksilver little Beatrice, — who at first said, "She had not the plague; only her cheeks burned; she should soon be well. Who had taken mother away?" However, she was soon won by Benedict's loving eye and tender hand. He chafed her limbs with oil; he administered his wonderful medicine; he threw open the back casement that looked toward the blue sea far away; he wrapped round her his own traveller's cloak. And in less than an hour the dear child looked up and said, "How I thank you: I am better;" and fell into a sweet sleep.

Scarcely had she uttered the words when a deep groan was heard from the couch of Guido: it was his last. Guido was dead.

And then Fra Benedict came again to Claude and said, "Your dear sister will recover: your brother is dead. Be persuaded: let me help you." And now Claude looked up with tears in his eyes and said, "Dear sir, have I not refused too long?"

But the good physician answered thoughtfully and calmly, "Be of good cheer, yet there is hope."

Yet had Claude reason dearly to repent the precious time he had lost. He took the medicine indeed; but it seemed at first only to aggravate his sufferings. The spasms of pain were so severe he could not help groaning and crying out in his misery. And sometimes delirium seized his brain. But Fra Benedict cooled his brow, and kept his hand upon the weak agitated pulse, until he felt it grow stronger and more regular beneath his touch. Then he knew the remedy was grappling with and mastering the disease. And so it proved. Claude fell into a perturbed slumber, which was broken with frequent starts and cries as of nightmare alarm. Still there were intervals of quiet, and they became longer.

In one of these, Fra Benedict hearing the bell of the dead cart again, quietly and reverently wrapped the father's best cloak around the lifeless body of Guido, and himself bore it to the door and laid it on that mournful bier. At another time he ministered food to Beatrice, who was now awake. Still he kept his eye on Claude, until at last he had the joy of seeing the beads of dewy perspiration on the boy's open noble brow, and the breathing became more regular: and Claude too sank into delicious and refreshing repose.

It were too long to tell all the tender care which Benedict bestowed on Beatrice and Claude. Though he had scores of other patients, he seemed especially to regard these two orphans as his own children. For the next three days they were very feeble, but he procured the choicest viands for them and the most cordial wines, until the color of health again flushed their cheeks. And then the good man told them, that while the plague continued in Genoa he would be to them as father and mother, and when he left them would provide that they should never want. And indeed they clung to him as if they had been his very own. They felt they owed him a debt which they could never repay; and one day Claude said so. But Benedict replied, "Dear children, would you try to requite me any thing I have done for you? The plague has yet been scarcely a fortnight in the city. It may have reached its height; but, if it tarries here as in other places, you cannot expect that it will subside for two months to come. Now I want to make you my messengers to other sufferers. You shall tell them what my medicine has done for you. They will believe you perhaps rather than myself. But I will never be far off from you, and you shall tell me every day all that you have said and done." The children gratefully promised to do what they could; and most touching it was to see them moving, like angels of mercy, among the sick and the dying. But I must not attempt here to narrate all that befell them during the next few weeks. Fra Benedict's work and theirs lay chiefly among the poor, though not altogether so. He was summoned again to Leonardi's house by the servant, whose life he had saved, to attend Lucrece, the merchant's eldest daughter, who fell sick the week after her father died; and though the attack was a very severe one, and the priests, strange to say, still opposed his attendance, Lucrece insisted on trying his remedy. She did so, and recovered. Her gratitude was intense. Also Giovanni's brother, Agathon, a princely patron of the fine arts, sent for him and was healed. But, as I said, Fra Benedict's chief work lay among the poor. One lone and aged woman, whom most men would have thought beneath their notice, he nursed as tenderly as if she had been a duchess, and gave Beatrice the most careful instructions for her comfort. And then a blind beggar, whose miserable existence seemed a weariness to himself and others, Fra Benedict wooed back to life, and often left under the care of Claude. And these also, like the children, he made his messengers and attendants upon other sufferers. It was surprising how many the blind man induced to send for his aid, and how tender a nurse the aged grandmother proved. More orphan children, too, were healed. And now the tidings spread from one to another, until every minute of every hour of the day was filled up with healing the sick or ministering to the convalescent.

It was a frequent marvel to others, whence Fra Benedict obtained his supplies of medicine and food. He appeared to be quite a poor man himself, and lived on the plainest diet, yet he never seemed at a loss to supply the wants of the sick and the suffering. Whether any wealthy friend of his in Genoa supplied him with large charity funds, as some maintained; or whether, as others thought, he had a secret store of jewels in his purse, was never known.

But one day the heavens were black with clouds and tempest. A heavy thunderstorm broke over the city. The rain descended in floods. The stagnant air was purified by incessant flashes of lightning. Fra Benedict's face was radiant with joy. He calmed the fears of the children, and assured them that the pestilence would now rapidly abate and soon pass away.

And he was right. The number of daily deaths, which had before fallen from thousands to hundreds, now sank to tens, and soon to threes and twos. The dead cart scarcely gleaned any victims in its long circuit. Those who had fled from the city returned. The deserted houses were reopened. The grass-grown streets were again trodden. The voice of joy and health was heard again in many homes, and the merry laughter of children once more greeted the ear of the passer-by. Ships again ventured from the Gulf of Genoa into the harbor. And after the lapse of another fortnight it was announced, in the market-place and in the churches, that the city was free from the plague.

Then a day of public thanksgiving was proclaimed; and it was ordered that all who had deserved well of their city in this its time of sorest calamity should repair to the council hall, and receive a medal of honor. Many a healed sufferer said Fra Benedict will assuredly receive the highest honor which Genoa can bestow. On the evening before the day of public rejoicing he stole quietly to the homes of those whom he had made his friends. They vainly urged him to present his claim on the morrow; but he answered mysteriously, "My presence is needed elsewhere: farewell." Leonardi's daughter Lucrece, at his request, undertook with tears of gratitude the guardianship of Beatrice; and Agathon, with joy, that of Claude. And then Benedict went among his own friends, and bade them adieu, saying, "We shall meet again in a city which no pestilence shall ever shadow, and where never a mourner's tear shall be dropped on the pavement of transparent gold. Till then, farewell."

And so it fell out: after midnight no man saw him more. Some thought that he went, as he came, in a little boat to a vessel lying off shore; others affirmed that a strange chariot was seen waiting after sunset outside the city gates; while others boldly maintained their belief that he was translated like Enoch. But as the citizens met in groups on the morrow morning, the question instinctively passed from lip to lip, " Was he not rightly named *Fra Benedict?* "

WHEN Oberlin laid down his manuscript, his grandchildren looked up silently for a few moments into his still speaking countenance, just as if he were in their eyes what Benedict had been to the orphans of Genoa. But the silence was broken by Robin the gardener (for whom Marie had pleaded a seat next herself at their Sunday evening readings), saying, "Well, that is the beautifullest story that ever I did hear: not that I know the meaning of all the words in it; still it went to my heart. But pray, sir, why was that kind-hearted doctor rightly called Fra Benedict?"

"Because," said Oberlin, "*Fra* means *brother*, and *Benedict* means *blessed;* and is not one who heals the sick a blessed brother to them?"

"Then, sir," eagerly asked Marie, "is not Fra Benedict in your story Jesus Christ?"

"Just so far," answered Oberlin, "as the Lord Jesus is the Good Physician of our souls. But we must remember that, while He is the Great and Good Physician, He employs thousands and thousands of His servants in the same work in every land; and they, too, are good physicians: only they derive all their skill and power from Him. But you have begun with the last words of my parable. Let us examine it a little more in order. Our time is very short; but this matters less, as the parable almost interprets itself. My little Röschen will tell us what that dreadful plague represents?"

"Sin, grandfather, is it not?" answered Röschen, "and all the sorrow that sin brings with it. But was there ever such a plague in Italy?"

"Indeed there was," said Oberlin, "in the year of our Lord 1348, too: nor did I exaggerate the numbers which Antoninus, Archbishop of Florence, said died in that city. But it was not confined to Italy only. In the course of a few years it overspread most of Europe."

"I read," said Adolphe, "not long ago, an account of the plague of London in the reign of Charles II.; that is hardly, you know, more than two hundred years ago, and I do not think any thing in grandfather's parable was more terrible than that history. I remember there, it was said, many became mad from terror, and threw themselves into the Thames. They had the same kind of 'dead-cart' going about to collect the bodies, the same kind of hospitals which they called 'pest houses,' the same deep trenches for burying the corpses. The grass grew then in the middle of what had been crowded streets. And the people thought they saw fearful signs in the heavens."

"But, grandfather," said Gustave, "surely people never were really so foolish as to think that building a hermitage outside the city walls would stop the plague. That you put in," he added archly, "did you not, to make up the parable?"

"You shall read us aloud, Gustave," replied Oberlin, "just one extract from a history of the plague which desolated Naples A. D. 1656 (reach me the sixteenth volume of the 'Encyclopædia Britannica'), that you may see I have not overdrawn the terrors and superstitions of a people who have not the Word of God in their hands, in such a visitation as the plague. There —"

[Gustave reads.] "'The distemper, being

neglected, made a most rapid and furious progress, and filled the whole city with consternation. The streets were crowded with confused processions, which served to spread the infection through all the quarters. The terror of the people increased their superstition; and it being reported that a certain nun had prophesied that the pestilence would cease upon building a hermitage for her sister nuns upon the hill of St. Martin, the edifice was immediately begun with the most ardent zeal. Persons of the highest quality strove who should perform the meanest offices; some loading themselves with beams, and others carrying baskets full of lime and nails, while persons of all ranks stripped themselves of their most valuable effects, which they threw into empty hogsheads placed in the streets to receive the charitable contributions. Their violent agitation and the increasing heats diffused the malady through the whole city, and the streets and the stairs of the churches were filled with the dead, the number of whom for some time of the month of July amounted daily to fifteen thousand. . . . A violent and plentiful rain falling about the middle of August, the distemper began to abate; and on December 8th the physicians made a solemn declaration that the city was entirely free from infection.'"

"Well," continued Oberlin, "there you have the dry facts of history; but I think you will find almost all the points of my story have some counterpart in the ravages of sin and the healing virtue of the Gospel. What does the Bible say about the close connection between sin and death?"

"Do you mean that text in the Romans, grandfather," said Adolphe, "where St. Paul says: 'By one man sin entered into the world, and death by sin; and so death passed upon all men, for that all have sinned;'[1] or that where St. James says, 'Every man is tempted when he is drawn away of his own lust, and enticed. Then when lust hath conceived it

[1] Rom. v. 12.

bringeth forth sin : and sin, when it is finished, bringeth forth death ? ' " [1]

" And you know," continued Aimée, " there is a terrible picture of a sinful land as smitten by disease, in the beginning of Isaiah: ' The whole head is sick, and the whole heart faint. From the soul of the foot even unto the head there is no soundness in it; but wounds and bruises and putrefying sores: they have not been closed, neither bound up, neither mollified with ointment.' " [2]

" They would not let them toll the bell lest it should frighten people more. What does that mean, grandfather?" asked Röschen.

" Well, my child," answered Oberlin, " the world says as little as it can about sin and death; but its silence does not alter the fact; the plague is there. Could any of you see a meaning in the different symptoms of the malady ? "

The children were silent, and Oberlin con-

[1] James i. 14, 15.   [2] Isa. i. 5, 6.

tinued: "You remember the pestilence sometimes attacked the throat, and sometimes the brain; in some cases it broke out with burning spots all over the body, and in others, while affecting the heart, was discernible only by a flush in the cheek and a wild lustre in the eye; but in all there was a craving thirst. Well, does not the love of sin seem so to choke some people that they cannot breathe the pure air of life, and makes others dizzy, so that they fall headlong, or cast themselves away? Does not sin break out in loathsome spots in some lives which all may see; and in others only appears by a strange excitement and unrest? But do not all alike thirst for a happiness they have not, and never can have, apart from Jesus Christ?"

"Oh, yes, grandfather," said Gustave, "but one thing puzzled me. I do not think that all bad people are so horribly selfish as those who left their sick friends to suffer and die alone. I am sure wicked people sometimes seem to me very kind to one another."

THE PLAGUE-STRICKEN CITY.   ·151

Oberlin smiled, and answered: "Thank God, you have not come across the path of many wicked people yet, Gustave. But you may take this for certain: the natural kindness of bad people who are kind (and I quite agree with you there are some such) does not come from their badness, but from better instincts not yet crushed in them. And those, who are called to deal with evil men, must always try and fasten on any of these good feelings, and make the most they can of them, while directing the sinner's eye to Jesus the only Saviour. But this, too, is certain,— that sin, so far as it gets possession of a man, shuts God out of the heart, and so shuts love out, for God is love. But our time is rapidly passing. What did you make, my children, of the helplessness of the Genoese physicians to cure those stricken of the plague?"

"I thought," said Marie, "of that poor woman of whom you read, sir, this morning, who 'had suffered many things of many physicians, and had spent all that she had, and was nothing bettered, but rather grew worse.'"[1]

"And I remembered," said Aimée, "that which always seems to me one of the most tearful texts in the Bible: 'Is there no balm in Gilead; is there no physician there? Why then is not the health of the daughter of my people recovered?'"[2]

"And see," said Adolphe, "here is a text, also in Jeremiah, which answers exactly: 'Thy bruise is incurable, and thy wound is grievous. There is none to plead thy cause, that thou mayest be bound up: thou hast no healing medicines.'"[3]

"Look on to the 17th verse of that chapter, Adolphe," interposed Oberlin, "and you will find the promise, 'I will restore health unto thee, and I will heal thee of thy wounds, saith the Lord.' What corresponds to this in our parable?"

All answered, "Why, this is just what Fra Benedict did."

[1] Mark v. 26.   [2] Jer. viii. 22.   [3] Jer. xxx. 12, 13.

"Yes, my children," Oberlin continued, "this is the blessed work of the Gospel, God's remedy for sin; that Gospel which tells of God our Father's forgiving love, and of God our Saviour dying on the cross for us, and of God the Holy Spirit making our hearts new and holy; that Gospel which was foreshadowed in the Old Testament, and preached by Jesus Christ Himself, and then committed by Him to His apostles and messengers; that Gospel which is freely offered to all without money and without price, which is especially welcomed by the poor, but which saves all who receive it. Our time will not suffer us to-night to compare all Fra Benedict's experiences with our Bibles; but we will talk of them during the week. And you will find how Leonardi, who trusted in his offerings to the hermitage and died miserably, while the poor man at his gate was cured, points out the superstitious man; how Rinaldo, the treasurer, who scorned a remedy which would cost him nothing, represents the proud man; how Lorenzo de' Medici, who thought his own potent drug would save him if any thing could, signifies the self-righteous man; and how Giovanni, who thought the remedy far too simple, is a type of the learned world, which in its wisdom esteems the Gospel to be foolishness. Then, further, you will see in the three orphan children a picture of three different classes of character: some, like Guido, have benumbed their powers and hardened their hearts, and perish in their sins: some, like Beatrice, are early and soon convinced of their guilt and need, and yield gratefully to the treatment of the Good Physician: while others, like Claude, for a long while refuse, so that sin gets a stronger grasp of their hearts, but yet, submitting at last to the Gospel, are saved through much suffering and many struggles. Then Claude and Beatrice, becoming messengers to other sick folk, remind us how all who have found the Lord Jesus themselves must tell others of His love. Also Lucrece and Agathon, being healed, speak of the few rich and noble who embrace the truth of the Gospel; while the forlorn old woman and the blind beggar, being raised from their misery and disease and employed in ministering to others, bid us not to despise or despair of any, for it is God's good pleasure often to take the poor from the dust and the beggar from the dunghill, and to set them among princes, and to make them inherit the throne of glory."[1]

There was a moment's pause, and Röschen said, " Grandfather, *had* Fra Benedict jewels in his purse?"

" The parable," answered Oberlin, smiling, " only said that this was never known; so how can I tell? This we know, that Jesus Christ never lets His servants want any thing that is really good. I can only suppose that Benedict's secret store was the promise, ' My God shall supply all your need according to His riches in glory in Christ Jesus.'"[2]

[1] 1 Sam. ii. 8.   [2] Phil. iv. 19.

"May I ask one question more?" said old Robin, humbly. "Why did not the good man wait a few hours more to receive the medal of honor? To my thinking he would have found it useful in other cities."

"Ah, my friend," replied Oberlin, "neither does the parable tell us this. This we know, our Master sought not honor of men; nor did His apostles snatch at the glories of this world; and the best saints of every age have been poor in spirit. The joy of Jesus Christ and of His servants is in the salvation of sinners and the glory of God. But grateful love is the truest wealth; and every true-hearted disciple is waiting his reward in the holy Jerusalem above, — that city of the living God which no pestilence can ever darken with the shadow of death."

EUGENE THE DEBTOR.

IN days of old, before the colossal empire of Rome bestrode the world, there was an extensive and fertile province in Asia, where every city with its surrounding towns and villages formed a little state or principality by itself. Some of these states did not number more than a few thousand inhabitants; but each had its own king, its own laws, its own usages, and not seldom its own costumes. The throne of royalty was usually the throne of judgment. The monarch not only wielded the sceptre and his sword, but all important causes were tried before him in person. His decision was final; there was no appeal. But the land having been originally colonized by Greek settlers, the names Solon, Lycurgus, Aristides, and other wise men of Greece overshadowed the minds of all; public opinion held the scales very equally, and injustice was rarely done.

In one of the largest of these states it was that Andronicus reigned. He was the father of his people. He and his only son Agathos lived not only in their own hospitable palace, but in the hearts of their people. It appeared that they only held power that they might use it for the advantage of others. The goodness of the king was in every one's lips. And yet he was inflexible in the administration of the just and liberal code of laws which he had himself drawn up for the government of his state. He never swerved to the right hand or to the left, for rich or poor. I say rich *or* poor; for the mother city of his realm lying on the sea coast, and having a brisk trade with foreign lands, poverty would have been unknown, but —

There is always a *but* in human history ; — there was a powerful and designing merchant, called Draco, whose only object, it seemed, was to amass immense wealth, and buy up all the houses and wharves and waste sites for building upon which he could lay his hands. For this end it was his wont to lend the unwary trader or the unsuspecting heir large sums of money at extravagant rates of interest; and then, if the gold were not repaid to the very day, he would come down upon the luckless defaulter like a vulture on a straying lamb, and claim the immediate forfeiture of the bond. There had been already many wrecks of noble families, the unhappy victims either languishing in the debtor's prison, or fleeing from justice, self-banished exiles from their native shore. It might have been thought that the sight of so much misery would have deterred others in the same city from falling into the same snares. But the headstrong passions of some, or with others the love of display, or the thirst for pleasure, or the fever of money-getting, drew them, as moths are drawn to the burning flame, into the clutches of the sleepless and rapacious Draco.

The king was deeply grieved. He did not think it right, for reasons of high state policy, to arrest the exacting money lender at present. The proofs of his injustice were accumulating, but they were not yet complete. The reckoning-day would come at last, and then Draco's ruin would be a terrible example to generations yet unborn. Moreover, his victims were in all cases themselves sorely to blame. Andronicus therefore waited, because he saw further than other men. But meanwhile he issued many royal letters, warning his subjects plainly of the dangers which they might otherwise incur unawares, and announcing the inevitable course of law, namely, that bonds and imprisonment awaited every condemned debtor till his debts should be discharged. These letters proved the salvation of many.

But there was a young man, named Eugene, of noble birth, who had been brought up at the most eminent school of the city, a school at which the king's son had himself been educated for a while, upon whom all the counsels of his parents and the disastrous falls of others, and even the entreaties of Agathos, seemed thrown away. The love of pleasure and of self-indulgence overmastered him. And yet there were some fine and generous traits in his character; and the royal prince had already more than once expressed his attachment to the ardent and impetuous Eugene.

Months and years passed by; Agathos had long since been called by Andronicus to share with him the weightier duties of royalty. And Eugene, after the death of his father, had come into the possession of wealth, which, though already impaired by his extravagance, was still amply sufficient to gratify every reasonable desire. But by degrees he threw off one restraint after another. Like the prodigal son described in the parable, he wasted his substance with riotous living. And then it was, alas! that he was open to the dark and insidious designs of Draco, who had long coveted the ancestral domains of his house. In an evil hour the hapless young man signed a ruinous bond, wherein he covenanted, for the immediate advance of a few thousand pieces of gold, to make over his mansion and lands to the usurer if the money were not repaid at fixed brief intervals. For a few short weeks he lived again in luxury and splendor, and then, being unable to pay the first instalment that was due, he was seized by Draco's orders in the midst of his indulgences, and dragged before the magistrates, and cast into prison.

The object of Draco, however, was the patriarchal inheritance of Eugene. For this a trial in the court of assize was necessary. A day was fixed. The king Andronicus sat on the seat of judgment. All who had any claims against the debtor were summoned.

And in truth the court was thronged with creditors; for the debts of the unhappy prisoner extended over a period of ten years and more.

The confusion depicted on Eugene's countenance grew deeper and deeper. There were many debts he had altogether forgotten, and which yet upon a single word being spoken flashed upon his recollection. And there were many things of which he was bitterly ashamed that they should ever be named before his fellow-citizens and his king. But nothing now could be hidden; claim after claim was substantiated; debt after debt was incontestably proved; yea, being asked whether he himself admitted the justice of the demands, Eugene could only answer: "It is useless to deny them; I am verily guilty; I can only throw myself on the mercy of my king."

But then Andronicus commanded one of the chief men of the city, who sat near him on the bench of judgment, to read aloud the statute which related to criminal debt and its punishment. And the statute was plain and unmistakable, and it ran thus: "Let the house of the debtor who is convicted in open court be sold, together with his wife and children, if he be a husband and father, and let the proceeds go to satisfy, so far as they will, the just claims of his creditors; and let the debtor himself be put in chains and kept in prison till the uttermost farthing of the debt be paid."

As these heavy words were slowly read aloud, the face of Draco assumed a settled cast of malignant satisfaction; but an irrepressible sigh of compassion broke from many in the court to see one so young, and born to nobler destiny, so miserably cast away.

Now, however, the king asked, as he was wont to do, whether the prisoner or his friends had any thing to urge in arrest of judgment, and said he would pause half an hour for a reply; but that, if nothing were alleged in that space, he would proceed to give sentence.

Oh, that terrible interval! This vision of his home and of his wife and innocent babes (for he had married one who was not unworthy of his father's position) flashed upon his mind, and then all the folly of his reckless course, and then the long interminable years of prison life which were before him. He felt faint and sick at heart, and a deadly paleness overspread his countenance.

But the minutes were slipping by. Half the time had passed. He looked with anxious, agitated glance around the crowded court. But as he did so, he felt that his case was alike helpless and hopeless. His debts were of such magnitude that none of his friends could even dream of discharging them. And the words broke almost unconsciously from his lips, "Woe is me! I am undone."

At this moment, when the king must in a few minutes more pronounce the sentence, and the notary-public was preparing to record the judgment in the register of the city, a voice was heard, "Make way for the prince;

Agathos is here." It was even so: and he advanced quickly but calmly through the crowd, which parted to the right hand and the left, until he stood beside his father's throne. A few earnest words passed between Andronicus and his son; no one heard the whispered sentences; but some said afterwards that they were narrowly watching the king's countenance the while, and saw a wonderful benevolence light up his eye and a tender smile play over his lip. But after the briefest pause Agathos, now facing the judge and now the prisoner, spoke as follows: —

"Father, I own that the sentence, which has been read from the statute-book of the city, is just. Eugene has heaped up debts which he can never pay, and has merited bonds and imprisonment. But, father, as thou knowest, I have loved that young man from of old. And thou lovest him, even as I love. His own folly and our common adversary have ruined him. He is undone. But love saves the lost. And, father, though it will

cost me one-half of that royal inheritance which thou hast given me, here in thy presence, and with thy approval, — for thou hast assured me it is thy good pleasure even as it is mine, — I undertake to pay poor Eugene's debts to the very last farthing and mite. Father, the payment is here."

At the prince's word a train of slaves entered into the court bearing bags of gold and caskets of jewels. Every creditor was summoned. Every claim was investigated. Every debt was paid then and there.

It were quite impossible to describe what feelings were passing in Eugene's mind, while these words fell from the lips of his prince and were made good before his eyes. He was struck dumb with wonder and gratitude. But when the last receipt was signed, and Agathos stepping up to him said, "Eugene, my friend, my brother, wilt thou accept these certificates which assure thee that thy debts are all paid?" it entirely broke him down; he threw himself at the feet of his prince, he bathed them with tears, and, while he fervently grasped the certificates and thrust them into his bosom, could only answer with a voice broken by sobs, " My prince, I have nothing but my worthless self to offer thee : but such as I am, I am thine for ever."

This memorable day, however, was not over yet. When the murmur of grateful applause in the court was with difficulty stilled, Agathos again advanced to the side of Andronicus, and said in the audience of all, " Father, the debts of Eugene are paid ; but he must not go forth from this court a penniless pauper. Half of my inheritance still remains to me ; and with part of it I here and now, before all, and with thy full sanction, O, my father, buy back all the property and estate which Eugene has from time to time alienated and sold ; and of this and of all the remainder of my wealth I make him joint-heir and joint-possessor with myself. If the title-deeds stood only in his name he might be tempted again to endanger or even forfeit them. I have, therefore, had them drawn in my name and his; but the free use and enjoyment of them shall belong to him as equal owner with myself. Here, Eugene, is the deed which makes thee with me rightful lord of this still magnificent inheritance. Only stretch forth thy hand and take it; all is thine, for I share all mine with thee."

To seize the parchment, and cast himself again at the prince's feet, and to exclaim, "O, princely Agathos, my life, and not my lips, must speak my love," was the irresistible prompting of the heart of Eugene. Nor was there a tearless eye in that crowded hall of justice (save only Draco's, whose baffled greed and malice were ill concealed by a scowl of defiance), when, to ratify the words which had been spoken and the covenant which had been made, the king took his signet-ring off his finger, and himself placed it on the right hand of Eugene in token of his adoption into the royal family. But they were tears of joy, and soon followed by exclamations of delight. For now Agathos threw his own purple cloak over his friend, and made him ride by his side in the royal chariot, and the shouts were taken up by the multitudes in the streets, as they together drove towards the mansion of Eugene. Only the prince suffered no one to go in with him while Eugene broke the glad tidings to his wife. She had been in an agony of apprehension. One look at his radiant face was enough. Let it suffice to say that her heart, with her husband's, and the hearts of their children as they grew up, were for ever knit to the prince and his royal father. In the few but deep words of Eugene, " Their life spoke their love."

NO sooner had Oberlin ceased reading than "old Robin," as the children called him, — though in truth he was but little over fifty years of age, and had three young bairns of his own, having married late in life after his honorable discharge from the army,—exclaimed, " Well, sir, I have seen a good deal of life, and heard more; but I must say I never saw or heard of a man doing like that young prince. I think men were kinder in those heathen times than they are in ours."

"No," said Marie, who had never taken her eyes off her master from the first word of the story to the last, "you are wrong there, Robin. Why, there's many and many a one among our French Protestant forefathers (I'm often proud to think their blood runs in my old veins) who laid down their lives for one another."

"That's true, Marie," answered Oberlin, " an ancestor of mine died, that a shepherd lad on his estate might escape. But we must take our story as it stands. A parable is something like a walnut: you must crack or open the shell, and then pick out the sweet, nutritious meat, here a bit and there a bit, a little fragment at a time. Let us now open our Bible, and see if it does not shed light on the eventful life of Eugene the debtor."

"Well, grandfather," said Gustave, "of course by the city and the state of which it was the capital our world is meant."

"And by its good laws and courts of justice," added Adolphe, "the righteous government of God."

"Yes," chimed in little Röschen, "I saw at once by Andronicus and Agathos his son we were to understand God our Father and Jesus Christ our Lord; and, grandfather, would not that psalm which I learned for you last week, the 8th Psalm, tell this, for it begins and ends with the same words, 'O Lord, our Lord, how excellent is Thy name in all the earth?'"

"It would, my child," replied Oberlin; "and then you know the Lord Jesus shares the throne of royalty with His Father, as He says, 'I have overcome, and am set down with my Father on His throne;'[1] and so it

[1] Rev. iii. 21.

is called afterwards 'the throne of God and of the Lamb.'"

"And that, I suppose," continued Aimée, "was what the parable intended by saying the king and his son reigned not only in their palace home, but in the hearts of their people; as when Jesus said to Mary at the sepulchre, 'I ascend to my Father and your Father, and to my God and your God.'"

"And then, of course," added Gustave, "that cruel and crafty trader, Draco, was the devil, who tries to make men sell their souls for the pleasures of sin, which are but for a season.[1] But I do not see, grandfather, how poverty could ever be unknown in this world. Almost all persons seem to me to be wanting something which they have not. I am sure I want a pony."

"Well, Gustave," said Oberlin, laughing, "you know the proverb, 'If wishes were horses, then beggars might ride.' Work hard, my boy, and you will very likely be

[1] Heb. xi. 25.

master of a horse one day. But to return to our parable: I quite admit that in the world as it is there is poverty enough, — I mean heart poverty, lack of the true riches which consist in the enjoyment of God's love and in the delight of serving Him. Only remember, no one need be really poor in these divine treasures, for God has blessed us with all spiritual blessings in heavenly places in Christ;[1] and as to earthly possessions, we read, 'Godliness with contentment is great gain (or merchandise, as the word might be rendered), for we brought nothing into this world, and it is certain we can carry nothing out; and having food and raiment, let us be therewith content'[2]— even without a pony, Gustave."

"Why does the devil desire man's inheritance?" asked Adolphe. "I have often wondered what use this world would be to a mighty spirit like the devil, even if he got possession of it."

[1] Eph. i. 3.   [2] 1 Tim. vi. 6–8.

"That is a deeper question," answered Oberlin, "than can be answered in five words or five volumes of words. It has exercised the minds of the deepest thinkers. But I believe it is a riddle that no one can fully explain on this side of the judgment-day. One thing we may safely say, the devil desires this world for his own inheritance, because it is Christ's inheritance. And the devil hates Christ with a fathomless hatred. It was the devil who stirred up the wicked husbandmen to say, when they saw the only and beloved son of the lord of the vineyard coming to claim the tribute of fruits, 'This is the heir: come let us kill him, and the inheritance shall be ours.'[1] However, we have to do with the solemn facts as they are. And this is certain, the devil does try by every means to make men waste their precious life here and lose their immortal life hereafter."

"Yes," said Röschen, "Marie taught me

[1] Mark xii. 6, 7.

that text last week: 'Be sober, be vigilant, because your adversary, the devil, goeth about as a roaring lion, seeking whom he may devour;'[1] for we had been talking of the three boys in our story 'Over the Hills Homeward,' and it is the most dreadful text in the Bible. I could hardly get to sleep at night for thinking of it. But why, grandfather, does not God shut up this roaring lion in an iron cage, like those we saw a year ago in the menagerie?"

"Because God's time is not yet come, my lamb," replied Oberlin, looking tenderly and fondly on the anxious face upturned to him. "But we are told in Rev. xx. that one day the devil will be seized and bound with a great chain, and cast into the bottomless pit for a thousand years, and then, shortly after that, will be cast into the lake of fire for ever and ever. 'God,' says Augustine, 'is patient, because He is eternal.' But meanwhile, whenever you think of Marie's text, think

[1] 1 Peter v. 8.

also of the promise of the Good Shepherd: 'My sheep shall never perish, neither shall any one pluck them out of my hand.'[1]

"Our parable," said Aimée, "told us the king did not think fit to arrest Draco immediately, and this because he saw further than other men. I suppose the royal letters he issued meant the warnings of the Bible."

"What a thousand pities it was," exclaimed Gustave, "that Eugene did not heed them! Backed as they were by the entreaties of his royal school-fellow, it really was unpardonable in him to act right in the teeth of them."

"And yet, Gustave," replied Oberlin, "the parable only etched what every one does who listens to the tempter and lives in sin; for the Bible tells him plainly, 'The way of transgressors is hard,'[2] and 'The wages of sin is death';[3] and more than all, the Lord Jesus,

---

[1] John x. 28.   [2] Prov. xiii. 15.   [3] Rom. vi. 23.

the king's son, who designed to learn obedience by the things which He suffered [1] in the same school our Father has appointed for us, entreats all to watch and pray lest they enter into temptation."

"Yes, grandfather," answered Gustave, "but it would be so different if we could actually see the crafty master, and hear the words of the prince, and go in and out before the king. Oh, I do so wish that we were really face to face with all these things! They seem so airy and dream-like."

"You want," said Oberlin, "that things unseen should be seen. You would leap into eternity without the education of time. No, my boy, we must now fight the good fight of faith, and faith is the evidence of things not seen." [2]

"Still, grandfather," urged Gustave, "it is so hard, it *seems* like fighting with shadows, though I know they are all real."

"They are real," said Oberlin earnestly.

[1] Heb. v. 8.   [2] Heb. xi. 1.

"Sin and Satan, and death and hell, are no shadows; nor, thank God, is life a shadow, nor Christ, nor holiness, nor heaven. But I am so glad you named, Gustave, how hard you find it to realize things invisible. For it is what we all find more or less. Some find it harder than others: but the harder the battle the greater the victory. Only remember, we cannot win in our own strength: we need and we have the promise of the Holy Spirit's help. What were the words, Aimée, you repeated this morning from Keble's lovely poem for the fourth Sunday after Easter?"

"You mean, grandfather,

> 'Swiftly and straight each tongue of flame
> Through cloud and breeze unwavering came,
> And darted to its place of rest,
> On some meek brow by Jesus bless'd.
> Nor fades it yet, that living gleam,
> And still those lambent lightnings stream;
> Where'er the Lord is there are they;
>   In every heart that gives them room,
> They light His altar every day,
>   Zeal to inflame and vice consume.

Soft as the plumes of Jesus' dove,
They nurse the soul to heavenly love;
The struggling spark of good within,
Just smother'd in the strife of sin,
They quicken to a timely glow,
The pure flame spreading high and low.
Said I, that prayer and faith were o'er ?
　　Nay, blessed Spirit! but by Thee
The Church's prayer finds wing to soar,
　　The Church's hope finds eyes to see.

Then, fainting soul, arise and sing;
Mount, but be sober on the wing;—
Mount up, for Heaven is won by prayer;
Be sober, for thou art not there.
Till death the weary spirit free,
Thy God hath said, 'Tis good for thee
To walk by faith and not by sight:
　　Take it on trust a little while;
Soon shalt thou read the mystery right
　　In the full sunshine of His smile.'"

"Thank you, my child," said Oberlin, "those words are always fresh. Here is the only hope for us all, old and young, even in the daily baptism of fire with which Jesus baptizes every faithful heart."

"But how, sir," asked Marie, "can the day of trial in the assize court be said to be now in this life? I always thought of standing before the judgment-seat after death, when this life's accounts were made up."

"That's quite true," answered Oberlin. "'It is appointed unto men once to die, and after this the judgment.'"[1]

"That is the judgment of the whole world after the general resurrection in the last day; but it is also true, that when God of His infinite mercy awakens a sinner to see his true condition now, He holds, as it were, His assize court in the heart; the soul is brought before His tribunal; He Himself sits on the judgment-seat; His holy law is the standard; the devil accuses; conscience and memory are witnesses; and the poor sinner cannot answer the judge one thing in a thousand, as the patriarch says,[2] 'Nay, in such an hour of solemn retrospect, when our past lies before us, and every hour condemns us, the poor sinner can but cry, I am verily guilty; I throw myself on the mercy of God.'"

[1] Heb. ix. 27.   [2] Job ix. 2, 3.

"And yet, dear sir," said Robin, "even that did not avail poor Eugene: he only heard chains and prison by law were the poor debtor's lot."

"And does the law of God hold out any hope to us, Robin?" replied Oberlin. "Adolphe, read to us Galatians iii. 10-13."

"'For as many as are of the works of the law are under the curse: for it is written, Cursed is every one that continueth not in all things which are written in the book of the law to do them. But that no man is justified by the law in the sight of God, it is evident; for the just shall live by faith, and the law is not of faith, but the man that doeth them shall live in them. Christ hath redeemed us from the curse of the law, being made a curse for us, for it is written, Cursed is every one that hangeth on a tree.'"

"Ah! my children," continued Oberlin, "here we have both the condemnation and the deliverance. But while that terrible curse is shadowing the soul, what peace or comfort

EUGENE THE DEBTOR.

can the convicted sinner have? will he not, like Eugene, think of all the happiness he has thrown away, and of all the dark sins which have stained his life, and of all the dreary prospect of an everlasting present, that prison from which Jesus says[1] the captive debtor shall never come out till he has paid the uttermost farthing? Can his friends help him? Can angels pay his debts for him? Nay, it costs more to redeem man's precious soul, so that men and angels must let that alone for ever."

"Oh! grandfather, I see it all now," cried little Röschen eagerly: "I thought I did before, but now I am sure. Jesus is our Agathos; He paid our debts by dying upon the cross."

"Is not this," added Adolphe, "what Elihu meant when he comforted Job? 'If there be a messenger with him, an interpreter, one among a thousand, to show unto man his uprightness: then he is gracious

[1] Matt. v. 26.

unto him, and saith, Deliver him from going down to the pit, I have found a ransom. . . . He looketh upon men, and if any say, I have sinned, and perverted that which was right, and it profited me not, he will deliver his soul from going into the pit, and his life shall see the light.'"[1]

"And then, brother," said Aimée, "this is made yet more plain in the New Testament, where St. John says: 'If any man sin, we have an advocate with the Father, Jesus Christ the righteous; and He is the propitiation for our sins.'"[2]

"Those two scriptures," said Oberlin, smiling, "are the warp and woof of my parable. Yes, the ransom price, even the inestimably precious blood of Jesus, satisfies every claim. His blood cleanses from all sin. And then, although we stand before the tribunal of infinite spotless justice, it is a Father's throne; and He loves us so as Himself to have planned with His only begotten Son

[1] Job xxxiii. 24-8. [2] 1 John ii. 2.

the way of our escape. I could only speak in the parable of Agathos giving half his inheritance in the payment of Eugene's debts, and the remainder as a joint portion for Eugene and himself. But, in fact, Jesus gave Himself altogether as ransom, and gives Himself altogether as the righteousness of His people, and their portion for ever. He is the Heir of all things, as we read, by His Father's appointment.[1] And, at the same time we know, 'As many as are led by the Spirit of God, they are the sons of God. For ye have not received the spirit of bondage again to fear; but ye have received the Spirit of adoption, whereby we cry, Abba, Father. The Spirit itself beareth witness with our spirit, that we are the children of God: and if children, then heirs, heirs of God, and joint-heirs with Christ.'[2] All we have to do is to stretch forth the hand of faith and accept the royal pardon, sealed with the king's seal and signed with the king's name; and again, to

---

[1] Heb. i. 2.   [2] Rom. viii. 14–16.

stretch forth the hand and take the title deeds of acceptance with God and of our heavenly inheritance, which are sealed with the same seal and signed with the same name."

"Oh! grandfather," said Adolphe, "I think the parable helps me to see more clearly, than ever I did before, how it is a free pardon on God's part, although the full redemption price is paid. For in this covenant between the king and his son all the debts of Eugene were paid to the very last mite, and yet no subject had any thing to do with the royal grace which pardoned and enriched the debtor."

"Quite so, Adolphe," answered Oberlin; "and in God's covenant of grace with man the freedom of divine mercy is yet more transparent; for while the Father gives the Son and the Son gives Himself to be the propitiation for our sins, so infinite and wonderful is the unity of essence between the Persons of the ever Blessed Trinity, that Jesus says:—'I and my Father are one;'

and in this great act of redeeming love the Holy Spirit, who proceeds from the Father and the Son, anointed the Lamb of God for His great sacrifice. Salvation comes straight from the heart of God to the heart of man. Man has only to receive it,—I say only to receive it; but when he has received it, then, like Eugene, his life, and not his lips alone, will prove his love. This great redemption will animate him for the great fight of faith, in which he will be more than conqueror, through Him that loved him, and will enjoy throughout eternity the glorious heritage promised to the victor. 'He that overcometh shall inherit all things, and I will be his Father, and he shall be my son.'"

PHAEDRUS AND PHILEMON.

THERE was a wealthy Savoyard nobleman, named Gaius, who was the owner of extensive lands lying at the foot of the Maritime Alps, some thirty miles inland from the opulent and learned city of Nicea, the modern Nice. He was of Greek extraction, and was the father of two boys, who were sixteen and fourteen years of age. The name of the elder was Phaedrus, of the younger Philemon.

The lot of that generation was cast in troublous times. There were wars and rumors of wars; and Nicea, lying on the confines of France and Italy, had been more than once occupied by the conqueror, as the coveted prize of victory. Now, however, for three years there had been a lull in the storm. The city was in the hands of the Duke of Savoy. And Gaius, who was a firm supporter of that royal house, and indeed a personal friend of the reigning duke, thought it a favorable opportunity to send his two beloved sons to Nicea for the benefit of the discipline and education of that noble academy, for which it was celebrated all along the shores of the Mediterranean.

It was not indeed without much solicitude that he determined on this course; as, having taken an active part in the political and military conflicts of the times, Gaius knew that his character was bitterly assailed by a large party in Nicea. His enemies, among whom Antidicus was conspicuous for the rancor of his hatred, were many and unscrupulous. If restrained from open violence, he believed they would do every thing in their power to seduce his boys from their filial reverence and loyalty. Moreover, there were not a few facts in his past administration of the affairs of the city — for Gaius had more than once held the office of deputy-governor, and had put down more than one civil outbreak with equal justice and mercy — which he could not fully explain to youths of so tender an age as Phaedrus and Philemon. Indeed, all the reasons of his conduct were only fully known by the duke himself. Gaius could not doubt that these things would be thrown in the teeth of his children.

On the other hand, he considered that a year's instruction would be of untold advantage to his sons, who, in his own retired castle, were almost shut out from intercourse with their comrades in age. He believed he could rely on their trustful allegiance: he knew that if he had many enemies he had also some faithful friends in Nicea, and especially one Philotheus, who had been brought up with him, and with whom, since he withdrew from the city, he kept up as constant a correspondence as the communications of those days allowed.

He called therefore his two sons, and addressed them as follows: "My beloved children, in whom your sainted mother, Irene, lives ever before me, and in whose boyhood I live life over again, I have thought it well to make arrangements for sending you to the academy at Nicea. You will there mingle with many hundred youths of your own age; some you will find friendly to our house, others hostile. Be courteous to all. While heartily returning the affection of those who love us, try to win others to our side. Much of your comfort will depend upon the clique of companions among whom you are thrown. But whatever they may prove, be you simple and truthful. Communicate freely with my friend and yours, Philotheus; and write me without reserve, whenever messengers come our way. Some things you hear may perplex you. I will not fail to answer your inquiries, so far as it is profitable for you to know at present. But for the full knowledge of some things you must be content to wait till you are older. Let *trust* be your watchword. Farewell."

Now these two boys, you must note, though the children of the same parents, and brought up in the same home, were of very different dispositions. Phaedrus, the elder, was grave, thoughtful, inquisitive; one who, from his very infancy, would always know a reason for every thing. "Why?" "How?" "What for?" were words constantly on his lips. He never forgot what was told him, but nothing escaped his eye. Philemon, on the other hand, was joyous and confiding almost to a fault, if that be possible. His frank, generous nature, as it never feared fraud, seemed as if it could not harbor suspicions of another. If the texture of his mind had not been so pure and upright, this would have laid him open to the intrigues of designing men. But, as it was, his very simplicity seemed his safeguard.

On their arrival in Nicea, the great master of the academy having examined the boys, assigned them different schools for their daily instruction, and different homes for their lodgment. This was a severe disappointment to the brothers, who, though so diverse in character, were passionately attached to each other. Yet it seemed as if a merciful Providence had overruled their respective places of abode.

Philemon — the young, confiding, impressionable Philemon — found himself in a school and home, where the larger number of the scholars and teachers and servants were well affected towards his father. The name of Gaius was seldom mentioned without honor. Sometimes indeed a slur was cast upon him; but before Philemon could reply, so many willing lips would defend him, that the slanderer was silenced and abashed. Philotheus was a frequent guest at the table of the officer in charge of the home; and he would often dwell in glowing terms of praise on the services which Gaius had rendered to Nicea and to the house of Savoy. And often was Philemon congratulated on being the son of such a sire. Thus as the boy grew in knowledge, he saw more and more to admire in his honored father's character and conduct; and, as his views expanded, he was increasingly struck with Gaius's firm and temperate administration when at the helm of the affairs of the city. His letters home naturally reflected all the delight which these things gave him, and those he received in return confirmed every conviction of his father's excellence.

Far different was the lot of Phaedrus. Every one in his lodgment, and almost every one in his class, seemed to dislike or distrust his father. For a while, whether from respect for the feelings of their new companion or from a deeper subtlety, they did not venture on open accusation. But when the name of Gaius was mentioned there would be an ominous silence, and stealthy looks would be exchanged between the scholars and their tutor. If any of the illustrious actions of Gaius were mentioned, there would be a faint ambiguous praise, which to the ears of Phaedrus was far worse than silence or downright condemnation. And when some difficult parts of his father's conduct of affairs was the topic of conversation, then suspicions would be freely thrown in, and sly innuendoes, or expressions of surprise and ill-suppressed ridicule, ending with an apparently honest appeal to the son for an explanation of things to him unknown.

Phaedrus was deeply grieved. He used often to say to himself, " Let them suspect as they like, and suggest what they will, I know that my father is just and benevolent and good." Yet the hateful suspicions, which he almost seemed to breathe in the air of his present abode, would recur at his quietest moments. If only his father had been at his side, he would not have minded. No doubt, he said to himself, his father would have resolved every perplexity. The next best thing was to write to him; and soon after this, hearing of a faithful messenger going and returning to his home, he wrote as fully as he could to his father of his difficulties, and prayed for an explanation of those acts which were chiefly maligned. But he was surprised to find how difficult it was to express in writing those harassing doubts, with which the enemies of Gaius plied him. When he would put them down in black and white, they seemed for the most part so cloudy and shapeless and impalpable, — it was like grasping a mist. However, he did his best: and, having confided his letter to the messenger, eagerly awaited a reply.

The answer was most loving and comforting. His father most tenderly sympathized with the mental sufferings of Phaedrus, and assured him that he valued the unshaken confidence of his son amid such temptations beyond all his other possessions. Also, in answer to his request, some further light was thrown on obscure passages of the past few years. But with regard to other events, Gaius reminded him of his parting words, "For the full knowledge of some things you must be content to wait." When, therefore, his comrades, who knew that he had received despatches from home, demanded what Gaius might say in self-defence, Phaedrus could only answer on many points, "I must take that on trust, and am willing to do so." Their laughter pealed through the vestibule.

Phaedrus and Philemon did not meet nearly so often as they would have desired, for their prescribed studies and games took up almost the entire day, and their dwelling-places lay apart. When they did meet it was generally in the presence of others; and even when they two were alone, Phaedrus felt a strange shyness from disclosing all his troubles and distress to Philemon. The brothers lived in different mental worlds.

One beautiful summer evening, however, having both obtained leave of absence from the officers in charge, they met alone in the cemetery which is situate on the hill overhanging Nicea. The eyes of both lads were attracted by the words inscribed over the portal, "Hodie mihi, cras tibi,"[1] and the solemn thought of another world, that world in which their beloved mother was awaiting them, drew out their hearts in all fraternal sympathies. And then Phaedrus told Philemon far more than he had ever done before of his inmost thoughts and struggles and endurances. Into much Philemon heartily entered, and repaid confidence with confidence. But as to any attacks upon their father troubling his peace of mind, he smiled at the idea of it. Suspicions rested on his heart like rain-drops on a cabbage-leaf; they did not penetrate a hair's-breadth. And Phaedrus soon forbore;

[1] "My lot to-day will be thine to-morrow."

he envied his brother's sunny faith; he inwardly accused himself of base unbelief, and almost experienced what a modern poet has described—

> "Yes, deep within, and deeper yet,
>   The rankling shaft of conscience hide;
> Quick let the swelling eye forget
>   The tears that in the heart abide.
> Calm be the voice, the aspect bold,
>   No shuddering pass o'er lip or brow;
> For why should innocence be told
>   The pangs that guilty spirit bow?
> The loving eye that watches thine
>   Close as the air that wraps thee round,
> Why in thy sorrow should it pine,
>   Since never of thy sin it found?"

However, they turned to other subjects, and then bent their footsteps to their sainted mother's tomb (she died at Nicea), and there, Philemon resting on Phaedrus, they stood silently and long; and as they returned to the city spoke only of their father's home on earth as a type of the one everlasting home in glory.

About a month after this Phaedrus had an

opportunity of a quiet hour alone with Philotheus in his studio; and, remembering his father's injunctions, he told him, though not without a great effort, of his present griefs. Here, indeed, he found "*an understanding friend.*" A single word was sufficient clue for Philotheus. He entered into every difficulty, as one who had himself struggled with the very same. He did not, it is true, explain all remaining obscurities. But his love and intense reverence for Gaius were so transparent, that Phaedrus felt all his own filial affection and esteem quickened and strengthened. And then Philotheus calmly showed how many things once dark were already clear, and advanced such cogent reasons why a veil might be drawn over other things for a while, that Phaedrus left his studio whispering to himself, "What a fool I was ever to let the accusations of foes disturb my peace for a moment!"

It must not, however, be supposed that his perplexities were ended from this hour.

They seemed to multiply as weeks rolled on. Altogether, different points in his father's administration were assailed, now covertly, now openly. And though he neither yielded to the insinuation nor the invective, — for, ever since his conversation with Philotheus, he had gained a vantage-ground which he never wholly lost, — it grieved him sorely that the name of his noble father should be thus traduced, and grieved him yet more that he could not clear it from every cloud. And now he began to be subjected to a thousand petty annoyances from his comrades. When the master's eye was off him, he would be vexatiously interrupted in his studies. His partnership would be declined in games, so that he was not seldom left to his own meditations. His rest would be wantonly disturbed at night, and he found it difficult to secure a quiet half hour, day by day, for devotion.

Haply his spirit would have sunk if it had not been for a young man of the name of

Ctesiphon, who, observing the ungenerous treatment to which Phaedrus was exposed, and his self-restrained and courteous deportment under all, began to conceive a strong affection for him. Though Ctesiphon had not the courage to declare himself as the ally of Phaedrus, yet he watched opportunities for intercourse with him, quietly frustrated many plots levelled against him, and befriended him secretly in a thousand ways. And truly Phaedrus had need of help.

One day things came to a crisis. It was a festival in the academy, and historic recitations were to take place before the chief men of that city. Antidicus, the bitterest enemy of Gaius, was present. And when one of the students had finished an oration on some of the last pages of the history of Nicea, Antidicus arose, and having thanked the young man for his glowing eulogium on their native city, he proceeded to represent the conduct of Gaius in the most sinister aspect;

he impugned his motives, he questioned his capacities, he accused him of serving himself, and not Nicea; and, finally, averred that the blood of many citizens lay at his door. Phaedrus could hardly restrain his indignation; his heart was hot and his cheeks burned; when suddenly Antidicus turned to him, saying, just as if he had been unaware of his presence before: "Ah! I see the son of Gaius is here. I rejoice that he is present, for doubtless he will explain, if any explanation be conceivable, the apparently crooked and disastrous government of his father."

Phaedrus arose, and as he rose the blood forsook his face; but, standing with his back to a pillar, he answered before all: "I do not know Antidicus, save by report as a bitter and unscrupulous enemy of our house. I do know my father as good, and wise, and just. Shall I let my ignorance master my knowledge? Is such the teaching of this learned academy? Far, far from it. With regard to the charges he now brings against my honored sire, many, as he knows, as you all know, have been answered again and again. For the refutation of the rest time only is needful. Truth is never afraid to wait."

Antidicus grew livid with rage. As the last sentence fell from the lips of Phaedrus, he muttered between his clenched teeth, "Does that beardless youth accuse me of falsehood?" At these words the hall became a scene of wild confusion. Phaedrus was seized and thrown on the marble pavement, and his gown rent from his shoulders, and many and grievous blows showered upon him. It is impossible to say where this would have stayed, had not Ctesiphon parried many of the thrusts, and Philotheus, coming in that instant, cast himself between the prostrate and bleeding youth and his assailants, and reproached them in indignant terms for the cowardly assault of many upon one, and that one only doing that which they

ought the rather to honor him for; namely, defending the reputation of a beloved and absent father.

The words of Philotheus recalled the young men to some sense of shame, and Phaedrus was allowed to retire, leaning on the arm of Ctesiphon; and when he had washed off some of the traces of the maltreatment he had endured, he made his way to the lodgement of his brother, who happened to be laid up with sickness that day, or he might have been exposed to the same insults in the common hall. As Philemon listened to the story of Phaedrus, and saw the wounds and bruises he had suffered for their father's sake, his heart was knit closer than ever to his brother.

From this day direct persecution became less and less. Many of his comrades in age were abashed by his courage and constancy, and a little band of four or five gathered round him. But yet the whole tone and spirit of the house remained unconquerably hostile to Gaius and his son. Time would fail me to tell of all the trials he endured, though they were now cheered by the companionship of his new associates, the occasional sight of his beloved brother, the steady friendship of Philotheus, and not unfrequent letters from his dear and honored father.

But now the year's probation was drawing to its close. Summer had long since given place to autumn, and the beautiful autumn sunsets had faded away, and the wintry frosts, though always tempered on that delightful coast, were yielding to the love of the early spring, when one day, as Phaedrus and Philemon were walking arm-in-arm through the cloisters of the academy, the well-known figure of Mnason, the old and faithful seneschal of their father's castle, was seen entering the portico. The young men ran to meet him, with the question of Joseph on their lips: "Is our father well?" Mnason, respectfully saluting them, answered, "He is well," and at the same time presented them with a letter sealed with the familiar signet. The letter was very brief: —

"My beloved sons, the courses of study, which I had it in my heart for you both to pursue, will come to a close on the evening of the day upon which you receive this message. I wish you to rise early on the morrow morning, and return home with Mnason in the chariot which I have sent for you. I have had constant reports of your fidelity and diligence. A hearty welcome awaits you from your longing father, GAIUS."

To bound up his own height into the air for joy was the instinctive action of Philemon, while Phaedrus heaved a sob of thankfulness from his inmost bosom, which seemed to roll off the burden of a year's anxieties and toil. However, they both grasped old Mnason's hands, and assured him they would be ready by daybreak. And then they hastened to bid adieu to Philotheus and their teachers and comrades. The parting was very tender between Ctesiphon and Phaedrus. Nor did they relax their embrace, until Ctesiphon had promised to visit the castle of Gaius, and learn to know the venerable man of whom he had heard so much.

The morning was without clouds. The orange groves and olive trees were dressed in the first verdure of spring. The larks sang a ceaseless matin song. And when the travellers glanced behind them, the Mediterranean stretched far away with its countless distances of blue, like an image of the eternal past. But before them was home, blessed home. Occasionally, indeed, a flush of anxiety might be detected on the countenance of Phaedrus, as he thought of the suspicions which he had allowed, even for an hour, to trouble his faith. But then the words of the letter which Mnason had brought, and of many previous messages from his father, recurred to his mind, and reassured him.

The horses, however, were fleet, and the

road was good; and as they surmounted the ridge of a wooded declivity, they saw the loved turrets of their castle home. Rapid as the chariot horses were, the young men's desires outstripped them, till, as they drew near the outermost watch-tower on their ancestral estate, they saw the reverend form of Gaius coming towards them, and caught the gleaming of his silvery hair in the sunlight, and recognized his beckoning hand of welcome. The chariot stopped a few paces from him, and the young men, springing out on either side, fell upon their aged father's neck and kissed him.

I must not linger to tell of all the joys of that happy day. This much I may say, that a few hours after they had arrived at home, and while Philemon was already wandering with inexpressible delight over the haunts of his boyhood, Gaius called his elder son into his own favorite turret chamber, and without one word or whisper of reproach for any passing doubt or fear, which might have clouded for a little while poor Phaedrus's peace during the past year, thanked him with all a father's tenderness and thoughtfulness for his persistent trust and loyalty and love. Nor was this all; for Gaius told him that he was now experienced enough to hear the secret reasons which had actuated his government of Nicea, when it seemed most open to censure. That very day many mysteries were cleared up, and Phaedrus was overjoyed to find how those things which looked darkest and most inexplicable were always the result of the ripest wisdom and far-seeing benevolence. Love to Nicea had been the master-key to all the conduct of Gaius, so that now his son began to rejoice in any mysteries that remained; for he knew that when unfolded they would only the more illustrate his father's providence and goodness. In a few weeks nothing was unsolved; so that one day, as Philemon was returning from the forest, Phaedrus, coming from the presence of his father, met him with the joyous exclamation, "O my brother, the darker the mystery the deeper the love."

"O GRANDFATHER!" said Aimée, as Oberlin laid down his paper and his spectacles, "I must add those last words, 'The darker the mystery the deeper the love,' to my book of *golden sayings.*"

(For you must know that each of the children, by Oberlin's special request, kept a manuscript book, in which they were accustomed to write down any good proverb or short pithy sentence which struck them in their lessons or at meal-time, when their grandfather would often read the daily journals aloud, or in their visits with him to the cottages of the poor. These books were labelled "Golden Sayings," and were read out from time to time in the happy family circle, affording bright subjects for table-talk.)

"Is it an old proverb, dear grandfather?"

continued Aimée, "or (looking archly at him) did you make it?"

"Well, my child," answered Oberlin, "I think the warp of it is as old as the Psalmist's words, 'Thy way is in the sea, and Thy path in the great waters, and Thy footsteps are not known,'[1] for God is love, and He works all things after the counsel of His own will; and yet how many things look very dark for a while which afterwards break into the brightest sunshine! We have very often now to trust Him when we cannot trace Him, and some things eternity only will explain. But if the warp of the saying you so like, Aimée, is as old as the Bible, perhaps our parable supplied the woof. Let us look at it a little more closely. You must not attempt to press every part of it into service, but its main features, I think, are plain."

"Of course," said Adolphe, "Phaedrus and Philemon represent different Christians, some of whom are sorely tried by tempta-

[1] Psalm lxxvii. 19.

tion, while others seem to know but little of it."

"And then, no doubt," said Gustave, "this life is the school, where Christ's disciples learn their hard lessons and buffet their way."

"And the world, I suppose," chimed in little Röschen, "answers to the great college at Nicea, where poor Phaedrus suffered so much."

"Then, of course," exclaimed Gustave, "Antidicus, the bitter enemy of Gaius, signifies the devil,—"

"And?—" said Oberlin, inquiringly.

There was a pause.

"And," continued Oberlin, "his servants and followers and agents. The devil does not approach us openly, as he did our Master in His great temptation, but he does stir up wicked men to tempt us, and plies his arts in a thousand covert ways."

"And then," said Aimée, hesitatingly, "I suppose, in the same sense, Philotheus represents all those good men, pastors and teachers and ministers, whom the Holy Spirit teaches, that they may teach us the things of God."

"Quite so, my child," replied Oberlin; "but what should you say was the main drift of my parable?"

After a little, Adolphe answered, "Would not the words of your text this morning, grandfather, express it better than any other, 'What I do thou knowest not now, but thou shalt know hereafter'? Though you dwelt so much on the story of Jesus washing His disciples' feet, and the lesson of lowly love to one another we are to learn from it, somehow I could not help connecting your text with the parable all the time you have been reading to us this evening."

Oberlin looked upon his grandson with beaming delight, and said, "You have indeed caught the spirit of my parable, Adolphe. As Gaius thought it good for his sons to go to the great academy at Nicea, though he well knew they would have to study diligently there, and would have to bear their daily cross, and be exposed to many hardships and snares and temptations, so our God and Father, who is training us for our heavenly home, though He knows we must learn many difficult lessons, and be exposed to many dangers, and often suffer much in enduring temptation, yet assigns us each one our lot in this present evil world, saying to us, 'All that will live godly in Christ Jesus shall suffer persecution;'[1] but at the same time putting that rich promise into our hands, 'Blessed is the man that endureth temptation; for, when he is tried, he shall receive the crown of life, which the Lord hath promised to them that love Him.'"[2]

"And yet, sir," said old Robin, "if I may make so bold as to speak, some men, and good men too, seem to go through life with very little trial or persecution. They are strong and hearty. No trouble comes nigh their dwellings. They live to a good old

[1] 2 Tim. iii. 12. [2] James i. 12.

age, and die in peace. Do they miss that blessing you speak of?"

"Well, Robin," said Oberlin, "I do not for a moment deny that some soldiers are called to far harder warfare, and will receive a brighter crown. One star will differ from another star in glory. But then we must remember, 'the heart knoweth its own bitterness,' and I have talked with many a one whose outward path seemed all that heart could wish, and found there was a secret trouble, sometimes a heart-trouble, sometimes a home-trouble, that the world knew not of; and I have gone from his house repeating to myself the words of our hymn, —

> "There are briars besetting every path
> That call for patient care;
> There is a cross in every lot,
> And an earnest need for prayer;
> But a lowly heart that leans on Thee
> Is happy anywhere."

"I've seen that, too, sir," said Marie. "But to put it in another way, was that young, trustful lad's a less honorable course than his elder brother's? My old heart quite went out towards that bright, joyous spirit."

"Perhaps," replied Oberlin, "we should not do quite wisely to compare one with another as to degrees of honor or happiness. God does not make all alike, and does not mean all to run the same course. Both Phaedrus and Philemon were faithful, though one suffered far more than the other, and therefore was the more qualified to enter into the reasons of his father's conduct. But 'the eye cannot say to the hand, I have no need of thee, nor again the head to the feet, I have no need of you.'[1] And we shall never know till glory who shall be first, and who last, among the disciples of the great Master. May God only grant us to be humble, diligent, trustful, hopeful scholars in the great school of life! He is testing us every hour."

"If life's lesson-books were actually put into our hands, grandfather," said Gustave, "like our Latin grammar and Virgil, and we

[1] 1 Cor. xii. 21.

were told that we had to master them in a given time, say in six or twelve months, and then be examined in them, it would seem so much easier. But it is so hard to feel you are at school all day and every day, especially when you cannot in the least tell when you may have to give an account how you have worked. Why, it may be fifty years or more before we are asked what we have done with our life."

"This is your old difficulty," said Oberlin, tenderly. "It is, I know, hard to walk by faith and not by sight. But this is God's discipline for us. There seem to me three great departments of that education which He assigns His children, — study, work, and trial. Often His scholars are passing through all at once. But with you, my children, the chief part of every day's duty now consists in study, the patient acquisition of knowledge, both earthly and heavenly knowledge. Now I know full well the lessons must sometimes seem hard and irksome. You have to take much on trust. But you will find the wisdom you are storing up now will stand you in good stead in after days. Then, as life goes on, most of your time will probably be taken up with work. You boys will have to earn your bread in some honest calling, and you girls will have plenty of happy homework every day. Yet we might soon perplex ourselves with asking why is it needful for a member of Christ, a child of God, and an inheritor of the kingdom of heaven, to be engaged often from morning till night in toil of body or brain. If tempted to ask this, let us remember God is trying us by these things of what mind and metal we are, — and those who are faithful in the least will be found faithful in much. And then along with study and work is mingled trial more or less all through life. We all in turn learn to suffer here."

Röschen colored up, and said, "I hardly know what suffering means, grandfather; except when I had that terrible toothache."

"And my little Röschen was then brave and patient," replied Oberlin, laying his hand on her head, "and gave good promise of being able to bear greater things for Jesus one day."

"Phaedrus's chief trouble," said Aimée, "seemed to be in resisting the cruel calumnies cast upon his father. But, since our Father is God, we cannot for a moment doubt that all He has done or is doing must be best."

An involuntary, low-breathed sigh that came from the heart of Adolphe told Oberlin that his parable had touched the secret trouble of one of his grandchildren. But he only replied, looking steadily round on all, "Yes, my children, we know that 'God is light, and in Him is no darkness at all.'[1] But it is also true, 'Clouds and darkness are round about Him,' and that He 'hath His way in the whirlwind and storm.'[2] And struggling faith often has to answer with Phaedrus, 'I know

---

[1] 1 John i. 5.   [2] Psalm xcvii. 2; Nahum i. 3.

that my Father is good; I will never let my ignorance master my knowledge; for the explanation of many things I will wait, and am content to wait.'"

Adolphe was glad to turn the subject then, though he fully resolved that he would pursue it some day when alone with his grandfather, and said, "And then, I suppose, we must number among the trials of life's school our being tempted by the devil to do what we know to be wrong, and leave undone what we know to be right?"

"And how did our Master meet such trials?" asked Oberlin, looking towards Marie and Robin.

"Why, sir, He met every temptation of the devil, as you showed us not long since," said Marie, "by the sword of the Spirit, saying, 'It is written,' and 'It is written again.' Ever since you preached that sermon, I've looked to my Bible for some sharp word to say to the tempter."

"And then," said Robin, "as to slighting

duty, He answered, 'I must work the works of Him that sent me, while it is day; the night cometh when no man can work.'[1] O, how often have those words nerved my tired arm and strengthened my failing knees!"

"Can you think of any other trials of our faith?" asked Oberlin.

"Oh, yes, grandfather," replied Aimée. "You mean the loss of those we love. How often you have taught us to plead the promises made to fatherless and motherless children! You have been more to us than we can ever tell, dear grandfather. But oh, I do long to see my mother again." And the loving girl's eyes filled with tears.

"Yes, my children," said Oberlin, "we are driven back and back to our text, 'What I do thou knowest not now, but thou shalt know hereafter.' We learn to spell out some of the reasons why God chastens us,—for in so chastening us He dealeth with us as with sons. But when the glad summons is sent

[1] John ix. 4.

us to come into His presence, when we see Him face to face, and dwell with Him at home. then shall that which is dark now be lighted up with the sunshine of His smile, and we shall joyfully confess He has led us by a right path to the many mansions of His love."

UNA THE BRIDE.

FAR off toward the golden sunrising, on the outskirts of the mighty empire of the king of kings, as Hammelech, not without reason, was usually styled,—for threescore and ten tributary thrones were wont to do him homage and held their sceptres at his pleasure,—was situate the small but most beautiful principality of Eden. It was a secluded valley, reaching only some thirty miles in length by ten in breadth, shut in by lofty snow-capped mountains on every side, from whence a thousand rivulets descended, and swelled the crystal river which flowed through its midst and found vent through the one rocky defile which gave access to the great world without. No tongue can describe the verdure of its pastures, the luxuriance of its flowers and fruits, the enchanting labyrinths of its forests and glens, nor the glory of those sunset hues that lingered on the peaks of virgin snow. Some say it was called Eden from its supposed likeness to the sinless paradise of our first parents; while others were bold enough to affirm, that this was without doubt that garden of delight in which God first walked with man.

Near the centre of the valley there was a tranquil lake of silver water, the banks of which were festooned with innumerable roses; and hard beside the lake, on a wooded cliff, arose the royal palace of the princes of Eden, who for many generations had reigned over the happy habitants of this vale. But, some fourteen years before my story begins, there had been gloom and mourning in the marble palace of Eden. Azrael, the angel of death, wrapped in the robe of that pestilence which walketh in darkness, had in one night borne away the queen-mother and her infant son, over whose birth there had been universal rejoicing but three days before. The king mastered his crushing sorrow before the eyes of his household; but the deep, deep wound bled inwardly, and in less than six months he was laid to rest beside his wife and babe.

And now the only heiress to this delightsome principality was the orphan Una, at that time a lovely innocent infant of four years old. All the hopes of Eden clustered around her. Dorcas and Deborah, widowed matrons of the highest rank, were appointed nurses of the royal child; and Perpetua and Felicitas, the twin children of Deborah, were ordered to be her playmates. Faithful soldiers guarded the palace gates and walls. And as she grew in years wise preceptors instructed her. Meanwhile, a reverend senate, consisting of four and twenty of the oldest and most trusted counsellors of her father, administered the affairs of the principality. Nor did Una disappoint the pains bestowed upon her, nor the fond hopes which her people cherished of her unfolding youth. Many anecdotes of her unselfish love, and many proofs of her ripening wisdom, were eagerly told from lip to lip, and were chronicled in the hearts of her future subjects. But it was whispered that she inherited the lofty spirit of her father, and his almost inflexible will. She did not seem to know the meaning of fear. From the age of ten years and upwards her delight was in threading the mazes of the forests, or climbing the rocky peaks to catch the rosy tints of the rising or the setting sun. In these rambles Felicitas was her chosen companion, and often did the woods echo to their innocent laughter. But not seldom, as she grew older, she entirely refused companionship, and would wander on in quiet thought, or bound like one of her own gazelles over the heather. And then it was her delight to visit alone the cottage of the fatherless and the widow, and to carry with her own hands the most delicious fruits of her palace gardens, melons or pomegranates or clustering grapes, to the bedside of the sick and suffering poor. It was in vain to argue with her; there was a calm self-possession which was a law unto itself.

For a long while, nothing of moment happened to break the quiet of the dwellers in the secluded valley of Eden. But shortly after the sixteenth birthday of Una had been celebrated with joyous festivities in every home, tidings were brought that Adonais, the only son of Hammelech, the mighty emperor of the east, of whose dominions Eden formed but the smallest fragment, had gained victory after victory in a terrible war with Alp Arslan, the rebel chieftain of a province lying far to the north of their valley. It was told how he had been severely wounded, but recovered, and rumor said that now, by his father's pleasure, Adonais had laid aside his military and royal state, and, disguised as a wayfaring man, was making a tour of inspection through the remoter parts of his vast empire. Many were the stories told of the unexpected visits he paid to the lowly shed of the peasant as well as to the mansions of the rich and noble.

Now some averred that Adonais had been seen to pass early one morning in the dusky twilight through the defile which guarded the entrance of the valley of Eden. But if it were so, he preserved his *incognito* most strictly the whole time of his sojourn there, for after the glimpses of that early dawn none of the inhabitants saw him again; and when some months had elapsed, certain information was brought that Adonais had returned to his father's court, and it was commonly reported that the emperor was designing an illustrious marriage for his beloved and only son.

Meanwhile, in Eden Una grew in gracefulness and graciousness. And not a few of the neighboring princes had preferred their suit for her hand to the counsellors of the little kingdom. She was as simple as a child; but whenever the subject was named to her she would listen with a courteous but apparently incredulous smile, and answer, she valued greatly the friendship of all her royal neighbors and allies, and plighted them her friendship in return, but with that they must be content. It was in vain to persuade her: you might as soon have moved the rock on which her palace was built.

Two years more had passed away, and Una was now the ripened maiden of eighteen summers, at which age, by the laws of Eden, the crown was placed upon her fair young brow, and she was proclaimed the sovereign of the principality of her father. On the evening of her coronation day tidings were brought to her, that a small but select embassy was on its way from the imperial court. Embassies were no unfrequent events, as

Hammelech was wont by them to keep up constant communications with the tributary kingdoms of his empire. But there was something about this embassy which, on its arrival at the capital of Eden, threw its inhabitants into anxious thoughts and many whispered deliberations. It consisted, not, as usual, of three counsellors, but of only one grave and thoughtful ambassador, whose name was Evangelist, a man who was known to have the emperor's ear as much as any member of his privy council; and he was accompanied by his wife Evangeline, in whose veins ran some of the noblest blood of the empire. Evangelist's only personal attendant was a venerable white-haired servant, whose name was Fidus; while in the train of Evangeline were three high-born maidens, Grace, Ancora, and Ruth. A commodious mansion near the palace gates was assigned them for their residence; and as Evangelist said his message was for the virgin queen's ear alone, Una signified her pleasure to give him audience on the morrow in the innermost court of her royal dwelling.

So on the morrow Evangelist and his little suite came to the palace; and when they were ushered in, Una, directing the others to remain just within the portal of the hall of audience, seated herself in a retired alcove, and beckoning Evangelist to approach, said that she was ready to hear the wishes of the emperor.

And upon this Evangelist began to plead the weighty suit entrusted to him. He told how the prince Adonais two years before had seen Una, when she had not the least suspicion that his eyes were upon her; how he had watched her gentle kindness to an orphan child who, but for her, must have perished with sickness and hunger; how he had traced her tender ministries, and heard her low-breathed songs as she sweetly soothed the broken slumbers of fever; and, further, how he had himself gleaned information regarding her from a thousand sources, and found that she was indeed one whom he could trust to share the administration of his mighty dominions. In a word, he offered her his heart and hand, and pleaded earnestly that she would consent to be his affianced bride.

Una listened with respectful deference to every word which fell from the lips of Evangelist, and after a short pause replied with all the courteous dignity of her race, that she was fully sensible of the high honor which Adonais, the son of Hammelech, the king of kings, designed for her; but that she was utterly unworthy of such distinguished favor, and utterly unfitted for such an exalted throne; and although she would take due time to consider her answer, she did not for a moment think that any alliance, however magnificent, would persuade her to leave the quiet seclusion of the palace of her fathers.

Evangelist thanked her for giving audience

thus far to his petition, and earnestly begged that he might be allowed ere long to renew his intercession on his lord's behalf, and urge many pleas which Adonais had commissioned him to employ. To this Una could not but consent, though it was with evident reluctance. And now, as glad to throw off an irksome subject, she invited Evangeline and her maidens in waiting to approach, and showed them some of the rarities of her palace home, and especially the almost matchless prospects which it commanded of the snow-clad mountains. For more than an hour they wandered through the costly apartments or gazed from the rose-twined balconies, and as they lingered, Evangeline, in the most simple, artless way, dropped many a word which seconded her husband's suit, saying how Adonais had often spoken to her in warmest admiration of these same beautiful views. Una said nothing in reply, but secretly marvelled when and where he had seen them.

However, after two days she sent again for Evangelist and his company, and told him that she had given his suit the most anxious deliberation; but that, having weighed it in the scales of a life-long choice, she had come to the conclusion that she must decline the imperial glory.

In the first place, she said, she could not bear to leave the scenes of her childhood. She knew every nook of the valley and almost every tree of the forests, every haunt of beauty and of grandeur, and every home of her beloved people. Then she confessed that she shrank from the majesty of Adonais. "I," she said, "compared with your noble prince, am a simple maiden, — the heiress of one of his most insignificant provinces; and he is the son of the king of kings. But in truth I prefer my lowliness to his magnificence." Nor did she conceal her dread of one who had been engaged in such mighty wars, and had passed through such scenes of bloodshed and alarm. And then, reserving the reason which perhaps weighed most with her for the last, she affirmed that she was unwilling to surrender her freedom, her heart and person, to another. She knew not that she should ever bestow her hand upon any suitor, certainly not for long years to come. She was my lady Will-be-will, and such it was her pleasure to remain.

Una added that she had consulted with two or three of her father's counsellors; and though they were taken with the glory of the proposed alliance, and felt their minds waver as to the advice they should tender her, they all agreed that it was a matter in which their royal princess must commune with her own heart and decide accordingly. She did not reveal that one of them had spoken disparagingly of Adonais, and avowed his conviction that her gentle love would be unsuitably matched with his fame for military exploits. But she said smilingly, though with something of a plaintive sadness in the tone of her voice, " Tell your noble prince how I thank him for his courtesy and tender thoughts of me: but let him seek some consort more fitted than his humble handmaiden to share the splendors of his imperial throne. For in sooth I can never be his bride."

Then Evangelist drew nearer; and by Una's permission Evangeline and her maidens disposed themselves near the footstool of the throne on which she reclined, whilst the ambassador pleaded his master's cause once more with wonderful skill, turning every objection she had made into a new persuasive argument for her compliance.

He began by reminding her that all her ancestral estates were really part of the dominion of the emperor; so that, although they were hers to inherit and enjoy, the suzerainty over them belonged to Hammelech and his house by an earlier and indefeasible right. He admitted the exquisite loveliness of her Eden; but he went on to describe the surpassing glories of Shushan, the palace, and of the imperial city, in such truthful and wonderful words, that the ear of Una was won, and she listened with inquisitive interest. Here Evangeline confirmed and enriched the description which her husband gave of the metropolis; and Ancora, one of her maidens, ventured to express a desire that the princess could only see it with her own eyes.

Furthermore, Evangelist urged that Una would not, by becoming the bride of the heir to the imperial throne, cease to be the crowned sovereign of her own peculiar principality. She would not lose her Eden by sharing the throne of Adonais in Shushan. Nay, doubtless the prince would often delight to return and wander with her over the haunts she so ardently loved. Only (and Evangelist again dwelt on the splendors of the imperial court) all these likewise would be hers, for it was in his commission to declare that all wherewith Hammelech endowed Adonais, with that would Adonais endow his chosen bride.

"Let the wealth of your noble prince be

as boundless as the universe," exclaimed Una, interrupting him; "the human heart was not made to love possessions, but a person. And I know not your Adonais, saving I have heard of him as a mighty conqueror. Magnificence would never attract me; so let us speak no more of it."

But just as if this reply had given him an opening to dwell on another aspect of the character of his beloved prince, Evangelist proceeded to give proof after proof of the tenderness and grace of Adonais. Evangeline threw in her glowing testimony, and appealed to Ruth to verify her statements, who told how she had seen him with his own hand ministering to his sick and wounded soldiers, and himself relieving the wants of the prisoner and captive. "It is true," continued the ambassador, "that Adonais has made mighty wars like David, but in his inmost heart he is a man of peace, like Solomon. Indeed, he only fought that his subjects might live every man under his own vine and fig-tree, none making them afraid. Had he not fought, illustrious Una, your beautiful valley would have been desolated with fire and sword, and, haply, chains hung around your tender limbs. It was your enemy he vanquished when he broke the power of Alp Arslan. And when himself sorely wounded in the fiercest crisis of that decisive battle, I heard him say that he considered his blood but the price he paid for the salvation of your Eden and of you."

Evangelist was proceeding to tell further of the goodness and liberality of Adonais to his attendants and ministers, "of which," he said, "I myself am proof," when Una, hastily gathering up her robes, as if she was afraid to listen any more, entreated him to forbear, for she would rather hear no more of one to whom, her heart told her, she could not surrender herself. So she withdrew, but not before she had granted the clinging request of Evangeline that they might present themselves before her in three days' time.

When next audience was given, Una seemed in the interval to have wellnigh steeled herself against further entreaty. She begged it as a favor of Evangelist that he should not urge another word in support of his suit. She loved her native valley, her beautiful home, Deborah and Dorcas, the nurses of her childhood, and Felicitas and Perpetua, the playmates of her youth, and her friends among the poor; but she did not and could not love one whom she had never seen. Let the embassy leave her, and depart in peace.

And then Evangelist made answer: "I will not further intercede myself on behalf of my prince, illustrious Una, if such is your pleasure. But Adonais charged me, if other pleas should fail, to give you this parchment written with his own hand. And Hammelech, the king of kings, sent you this portrait of his only and beloved son."

The parchment was closely folded, and sealed with the signet which Adonais always wore on his right hand, of which the device was a rescued lamb in the shepherd's arms. And the portrait was the cunning work of the subtlest artist in the kingdom, and was set all in gold and rubies, telling of the burning love of him whose noble countenance it delineated.

Una took the portrait with a trembling hand (no one had ever seen that hand shake till now), and placed it on the porphyry table before her, and gazed on it at first dreamily, but soon more intently; and then she took the parchment and held it a long while unopened; but at last, as one musing or amazed, she broke the seal and began to read, line after line, and sentence after sentence. No one ever knew all that was written there save herself. Only as she caught the meaning of the words her eye was moistened with tenderness, and before she had read one half she could not see clearly for the mist of tears. So she laid the parchment down and gazed again upon the portrait.

And it seemed she was utterly unconscious of the presence of Evangelist and Fidus, and of Evangeline and her maidens. For anon she read another sentence, and then again looked wistfully at the portrait; and then again she read on and on. But when she came to the closing words, " I sign my letter in my own blood, blood that flowed from a deep wound received in a battle fought, Una, for thy sake, and which may assure thee I love thee unto death, and am for ever and for ever thine own Adonais," Una restrained herself no more; she leaned her head on the bosom of Grace, who at the moment seemed instinctively to draw near to her side, and wept silently and long.

Hardly half an hour had passed away, before Evangelist broke the stillness by asking whether Una would now grant him permission again to urge his beloved master's suit. But she answered in a low, sweet voice, " Thy master's suit is granted," and gave the ambassador her little snow-white hand in token of the royal word having passed her lips. Evangelist respectfully grasped it in both his hands, looking up to heaven in overflowing thankfulness, and, having pressed it once and again to his lips, he took from the purse in his girdle a ring of priceless value with which Adonais had entrusted him, and placed it on Una's finger as the ring of betrothal. Then at his beck Fidus approached, bearing a casket of pearls and gems, such as Eden had never known, for the household of the princess. So Una summoned Dorcas and Deborah, with her lovely twin girls, and herself fastened around their neck and wrists these jewels of dazzling beauty, telling them in broken whispers how she had pledged her heart and hand to Adonais. And meanwhile the three handmaidens of Evangeline at her request touched their silvery lutes, and sung the most exquisite song which Una had ever heard. The words and the music alike were composed by the prince himself, who was a lyrist of no mean order, and the burden of it was, "Rise up, my love, my fair one, and come away; for, lo, the winter is past, the rain is over and gone, the flowers appear on the earth, the time of the singing of birds is come, and the voice of the turtle is heard in the land. Arise, my love, my fair one, and come away." And Evangelist and Evangeline, as if now they were permitted to speak on Una's behalf, sang right nobly in response, "My beloved is mine, and I am his; he feedeth among the lilies. Until the day break and the shadows flee away, turn, my beloved: and be thou like a roe or young hart upon the mountains of Bether."[1]

The sun had not set behind the western hills before Fidus was despatched to bear the glad tidings of Una's consent to the imperial court. At least one moon must wax and wane before with the utmost speed an answer could be received. Now, it is worthy of note that Una was never for doing things by

[1] *Bether*, which, being interpreted, is "division."

halves. She was like the cloud of the poet,
"Which moveth altogether if it move at all;"
and she therefore joyfully anticipated that the prince would immediately either send his chosen body-guard to escort her to Shushan, or himself come with the quick footsteps of love to claim his bride in Eden.

But the reply was brought by Fidus to Evangelist. It was in the form of a letter addressed to the ambassador, containing a sealed inclosure for the princess. Both communications were in the handwriting of Adonais. Una thrust hers into the folds of her garment, and retired into her innermost chamber to read it. The letter was long. It began with assurances of holy and tender delight (a delight altogether shared by Hammelech his father) in the pledged affection of his beautiful betrothed princess. It went on to tell of the ardent love with which he had watched over her childhood and early youth, when she had scarcely heard his name. It alluded, though briefly, to the mighty wars he had waged in defence of her sequestered Eden. And then it narrated with what ardent anxiety he awaited the success of the mission of Evangelist, how he rejoiced with joy unspeakable at the tidings brought by Fidus, and how he embraced her with all his heart, and should esteem their bridal as the crown of his every hope. But it went on to say, that the rebels in the province to the north of Eden were not yet altogether put down. The foe had been indeed utterly routed in that pitched battle wherein Adonais himself had been so sorely wounded, but the rebellious troops, though scattered, were not destroyed. Alp Arslan had broken prison, and was ranging to and fro with intent to band them in a new confederacy. Hence Adonais wrote that he was unwilling to claim Una as his bride with his military task not wholly accomplished. He could not bear the thought that Alp Arslan in his madness might even attempt to mar their marriage festivities. He therefore proposed (and this was his father's good pleasure too), first to crush the still smouldering embers of this rebellion, to storm every mountain fastness of the foe, and not to rest till he had taken Alp Arslan captive again, and sent him in chains to the imperial dungeon, from whence escape was hopeless. He could not absolutely fix the term of the war: it should be as short as love could make it. But, meanwhile, he longed that his Una should yet further prepare herself for the vast responsibilities that were before her as the future empress of the greatest monarchy in the world. He tenderly intimated that she was still but young, and that one who had so lovingly promised to be his equal partner for life should be able to sympathize with all his interests and pursuits. He said that Evangelist and Evangeline knew his mind, and would glady give their counsel whenever she demanded it. He further said that he was building for her a palatial mansion, adorned with gold and silver and precious stones, within the walls of Shushan, which would eclipse every other in the universe. And he concluded by dwelling on the long happy years they might hope to spend in that mansion, interspersed with not unfrequent visits to her native Eden, years of holy union, which should be none the less fruitful in abiding joy for the delay which intervened before the accomplishment of his heart's desire.

As Una finished reading this letter she heaved an involuntary sigh from the very bottom of her heart. For though at first she so greatly shrank from leaving her native valley, and entrusting her happiness to the custody of the prince, even as I have narrated, yet now that her choice was made and her affections won, she could hardly brook delay. She could not, however, but admit the wisdom of Adonais's resolve. She said to herself, it must cost him even more than it costs me; for he has seen the one whom he is pleased to love, whereas I have only seen his portrait and read his dear words of affection; and yet he deems it best to postpone our bridal. Then she rejoiced to think with what confidence Adonais wrote of putting all his enemies under his feet. And lastly, she dwelt with peculiar delight on his words, that the interval should be as short as love could make it. So, early on the morrow she sent for Evangelist, and set herself in right earnest to fulfil the good pleasure of the prince.

The interval, indeed, proved far longer than she had thought. But the studies which Evangelist suggested, and which she pursued with Evangeline, were in themselves so intensely interesting, and bore so evidently on her future exalted lot, that often the day seemed hardly long enough for its manifold claims. The affairs of her own principality demanded often serious attention; nor would she altogether forego her favorite rambles through the forests, nor her visits to the poor. Still there were many moments, even in her busiest days, in which her thoughts flew to Adonais like a dove to its nest. And the irrepressible question rose to her lips, why tarry the wheels of his chariot?

Many things would set her a longing;— if she did but hear the prince's name; if she did but touch the betrothal ring on her finger; if her eyes did but fall on his portrait; if Evangelist discoursed of his wisdom, or Evangeline and her maidens sang, as they were wont to do, of his excellent glory; if, as not seldom, she received some choice token of affection from him, some jewel which he had purchased, or some banner which he had conquered in the war, or haply a letter written with his own hand telling of his victories and nearer advent,— then, as aforesaid, she felt a longing, and was overheard more than once, even in her dreams, to say, "Come quickly, my beloved, come."

But at length, when hope deferred had become a strange habitual craving of heart, —for two years had already passed, and the joyous springtide of the third year was gladdening the eye with beauty and refreshing the ear with song, — there came a post late one night with a letter from the prince himself to Una, telling her that after many wearisome marches he had overtaken and overcome the last troops of the enemy, that Alp Arslan was in chains once more, that the mansion in Shushan was completed, and begging her to come to meet him just beyond the frontier defile of Eden on the morrow.

As Evangelist had always told her that, from what he knew of the prince's character and purpose, the announcement of his coming would be sudden at last, she was not taken by surprise. It was nothing but joyous delight. All was in readiness. The affairs of Eden were despatched with a few words. The arrangements of her home were complete. Her choice jewels, save only her betrothal ring, were soon distributed among her early friends; for Adonais had begged it as a special favor that she would expect her bridal adornments from the imperial city. So her chariot horses were soon caparisoned, and very early in the morning she was on her way. The air was breezy with the blessings of her affectionate people. Dorcas and Deborah, with her children, Perpetua and Felicitas, accompanied her to the entrance of the mountain pass, where they resigned her to the care of Evangelist and his suite.

As she was passing through the defile another embassy from the imperial court met her, bearing bridal gifts from the king of kings, and Evangeline and her maidens arrayed the lovely Una in far more beautiful garments and jewels than she had ever dreamed of before. Yet in truth at that hour she scarcely bestowed a passing thought upon them, for she was continually asking herself, where is Adonais?

At length, however, she emerged from the shadow of the defile into the spacious plain beyond, and there, far as the eye could reach, stretched the magnificent army of the prince. In the centre was pitched his royal pavilion, and over it the imperial standard, with its peace device of lilies interwoven with roses floating on the wind. But now, as messenger after messenger met her chariot, Una drooped her bridal veil to hide the burning blushes of her joy. And at last the cry was heard, "The prince, the prince! long live Adonais!" And in truth it was he. And the clarions sounded, and the trumpets rang, and the air was rent with military music.

But who shall rightly describe the beauty and the glory of the prince, the calm majesty of his beaming countenance, the nobility of his brow, the penetrating glance of his eye, and the deep melody of his voice? He was in truth the idol of his soldiers, and was surrounded by a brilliant staff of officers. But as he waved his hand they fell off from him on either side, and his bosom friend alone rode forward and whispered to Evangelist, that it was the prince's desire that Una should alight and meet him alone. With stately grace she descended from her chariot, and fifty paces further on, the royal bridegroom met the bride of his heart. His hand lifted her transparent veil. His lips met hers. She would have sunk to the earth, but he caught and clasped her to his bosom, saying, "Thou art mine;" and she answered in the words which she had caught from Evangeline's song, "My beloved is mine, and I am his."

The nuptials were celebrated that day in the presence of the rejoicing army; and the prince led his lovely bride to his royal pavilion amid shouts of welcome so loud that the earth rang again to the echoes of "Long live Adonais! long live Una!" For three days, such was their leader's command, the soldiers celebrated the auspicious spousal in festivities throughout the camp, and then Adonais ordered that the mighty host should turn their standards homewards;— so

"Now the soft peace-march beats, Home, brothers, home;"

and by easy stages at last they arrived before the walls of Shushan, the palace. There the prince presented his beautiful bride to Hammelech his father, who was no less delighted with the modesty of her wisdom than with the surpassing loveliness of her countenance. As the three discoursed a long while on various topics of imperial moment, and Una found herself able to enter intelligently and with graceful ease into every question, how glad was she in her heart of the diligent use to which she had put the weary interval of delay before her bridal!

And from his father's palace Adonais led her with joyous expectations to his own, that peerless mansion which he had himself devised and builded for her dwelling-place, and every part of which was furnished by his express directions for her entertainment and delight. And in truth, as she wandered from room to room, or reclined beside the cool fountains in the hanging gardens, which recalled all her dreams of Paradise, she found herself repeating unconsciously the words which fell from the lips of Sheba's queen in the presence of

Solomon: "It was a true report that I heard in mine own land of thy acts and of thy wisdom; howbeit I believed not the words until I came and mine eyes had seen it; and behold the half was not told me."

The city was beautiful, the palace was beautiful, the gardens were beautiful. But far, far beyond all other delights was her communion with Adonais himself. His glory and his grace satisfied every longing of her heart. And when Evangeline ventured to ask her what now she thought of her spouse, she could only make reply, "My beloved is the chiefest among ten thousand; yea, he is altogether lovely: and he is mine, and I am his, for ever and for ever."

I may not pursue the story. But I heard that in after years Una became the joyful mother of children, whom she made princes in all lands, and that one of her sons reigned as her viceroy, the lord regent of Eden. There was constant and uninterrupted communication between her native valley and

Shushan the palace; and it was admitted by universal consent, that the secluded principality of Eden was the favorite retreat of Adonais and his household.

NOW Oberlin, having come to the end of his story, did not wait to be questioned by the eager opening lips of his grandchildren; but, before they could speak a word, he continued: "I will read you, my children, the verses of that poem which first gave me the thought of my parable, because I think they explain in very few and very beautiful words the meaning of much of that story which I see has so interested you. The poem is called 'The Soul of Man, and the Immortality Thereof,' and was written by Sir John Davies, an eminent lawyer in Queen Elizabeth's reign. Indeed, the poem was dedicated to her, and first appeared in the year of our Lord 1599. He is proving the divine origin of the soul:—

'Which in this earthly mold
  The Spirit of God doth secretlie infuse,
Because at first she doth the earth behould,
  And onely this materiall world she viewes ;

'At first our mother-earth shee holdeth dere,
  And doth embrace the world and worldly things ;
She flyes close by the ground and houers here,
  And mounts not vp with her celestiall wings :

'Yet vnder heauen shee cannot light on ought
  That with her heauenly nature doth agree ;
She cannot rest, she cannot fix her thought,
  She cannot in this world contented be.'

And after a few verses of like argument, Sir John Davies goes on. (I do not think there are any old English words which will puzzle you, though perhaps the spelling might.)

'Sith then her heauenly kind shee doth bewray,
  In that to God she doth directly moue,
And on no mortall thing can make her stay,
  She cannot be from hence, but from aboue.

'And yet this first true cause and last good end,
  She cannot heere so well and truly see :
For this perfection she must yet attend,
  Till to her Maker shee espoused bee.

'As a king's daughter, being in person sought
    Of diuerse princes which do neighbour neare,
On none of them can fixe a constant thought,
    Though shee to all doe lend a gentle eare;

'Yet can she loue a forraine emperour
    Whom of great worth and powre she heares to be,
If she be woo'd but by ambassadour,
    Or but his letters or his pictures see;

'For well she knows that, when she shal be brought
    Into the kingdome where her spouse doth raigne,
Her eyes shall see what shee conceiu'd in thought,
    Himselfe, his state, his glorie, and his traine.

'So, while the virgin soule on earth doth stay,
    She woo'd and tempted is ten thousand wayes
By those great powers, which on the earth beare sway
    The wisdome of the world, wealth, pleasure, praise:

" With these sometime she doth her time beguile,
    These do by fits her phantasie possesse,
But she distasts them all within a while,
    And in the sweetest finds a tediousnesse.

'But if vpon the world's Almightie King
    She once doe fixe her humble, louing thought,
Who by his picture drawne in euery thing
    And sacred messages her loue hath sought;

'Of him she thinks she cannot thinke too much;
    This hony tasted still is euer sweete;
The pleasure of her rauisht thought is such,
    As almost here she with her blisse doth meete.

' But when in heauen she shall his Essence see,
  This is her soueraigne good and perfect blisse;
 Her longings, wishings, hopes, all finisht bee,
  Her ioyes are full, her motions rest in this :

' There is she crownd with garlands of content;
  There doth she manna eate and nectar drinke ;
 That presence doth such high delights present,
  As neuer tongue could speake, nor hart could thinke.' "

As Oberlin laid down the choice antique little volume from which he read this fragment, old Robin could contain himself no more, but lifted up his hands in amazement, exclaiming, "Well, sir, that is perfectly delightful. It not only takes me back to the days in which I courted my Jean, — and you know, sir, she had to wait five years for me while I was in the Indies, — but someway, I cannot tell how, this parable of yours, sir, seems to make all our life one long love-story."

"And yet," said Oberlin, "have we not abundant warrant in Scripture for picturing God's love to us under the similitude of a bridegroom's love to the bride ? Cannot my children give me proofs of this from their Bibles?"

"I thought of the words," answered Aimée, "'Hearken, O daughter, and consider, and incline thine ear; forget also thine own people and thy father's house; so shall the King greatly desire thy beauty; for He is thy Lord, and worship thou Him.'"[1]

"And I," said Gustave, "of the verses we learnt after hearing Avehdah, 'Thou shalt no more be termed forsaken, neither shall thy land any more be termed desolate. But thou shalt be called Hephzibah, and thy land Beulah; for the Lord delighteth in thee, and thy land shall be married.'[2] And I remember the next verse went on to say, 'As the bridegroom rejoiceth over the bride, so shall thy God rejoice over thee.'"

"I could only think," said Röschen, "of the parable of Jesus; but you know He said, 'The kingdom of heaven is like unto a certain king, who made a marriage for his son.'"[3]

[1] Psalm xlv. 10, 11.   [2] Isa. lxii. 5.   [3] Matt. xxii. 2.

"Have you a verse, Adolphe?" asked Oberlin.

"Well, grandfather," replied Adolphe, "I was turning over in my mind those words you read in church this afternoon. Here they are:—'Husbands, love your wives, even as Christ also loved the church, and gave Himself for it, that He might sanctify and cleanse it with the water by the word, that He might present it to Himself a glorious church, not having spot, or wrinkle, or any such thing; but that it should be holy and without blemish. So ought men to love their wives as their own bodies. He that loveth his wife loveth himself. For no man ever yet hated his own flesh, but nourisheth and cherisheth it, even as the Lord the church.'[1] But when you read those verses by Sir John Davies I was puzzled, for he seems to speak of the soul, and the Bible to speak of the whole church, being the bride."

"I do not think," said Oberlin, "that this

[1] Eph. v. 25–29.

perplexity need disturb our enjoyment of the figure, nor our interpretation of the parable. Let us remember what St. Paul said to the Corinthian Christians: 'I am jealous over you with godly jealousy, for I have espoused you to one husband, that I may present you as a chaste virgin to Christ.'[1] There he speaks of the believers in Corinth as the bride, yet they were in truth but a very small part of Christ's mystical body. It is so with other figures. Take that of a temple. Sometimes each saint is said to be God's temple, sometimes each Christian church, sometimes the holy church universal in heaven and earth. So is every member of the spouse of Christ spoken of as His bride, and each and all may say, in the language of the Song of Solomon, 'I am my Beloved's, and my Beloved is mine.'[2] Until, at last, the perfect unity of the church shall be seen, when the marriage of the Lamb is come, and His wife shall have made herself ready."[3]

[1] 2 Cor. xi. 2.   [2] Song vi. 3.   [3] Rev. xix. 7.

"Then, grandfather," said Adolphe, "another difficulty struck me. Una was so good; a little wayward, perhaps, but oh, so good and gentle and kind before Adonais sought her hand. And you have always taught us from the Bible that the heart is evil, until Jesus makes it His own."

"Dear boy," answered Oberlin, "yours is a thoughtful difficulty, but I have often told you we must not expect to get the whole round of Gospel teaching from one parable. We must be content if each figure sets forth one aspect of it. Some of our other parables taught us plainly enough the sin and misery of man before the grace of God visits him. I need but remind you of the Reef, or Avehdah, or Over the Hills Homeward, or the Plague-stricken City, or Eugene the Debtor. The great object of our story, this evening, is to picture forth the love of Jesus to us at last awakening our love to Him, as in His own gracious words, 'Ye have not chosen me, but I have chosen you, and ordained you that ye should go and bring forth fruit, and that your fruit should remain, that whatsoever ye shall ask of the Father, He may give it you.'"[1]

"Would not my morning text, grandfather," asked little Röschen, "say this too, 'We love Him because he first loved us'?"[2]

"It would, my lamb," answered Oberlin. "That is the key to our life's long love-story, as Robin called it just now, and I think you will find with this key that almost every sentence of my parable expresses some spiritual truth. Could you make out the meaning of the names, my children?"

"Not all, grandfather," said Aimée, "but I suppose Una means 'only,' and so 'only beloved,' for I observed the other day, when Solomon says, 'I was tender and only *beloved* in the sight of my mother,'[3] the word *beloved* is in italics, and that would leave 'only' by itself. Then, of course, her playmates, Perpetua and Felicitas, mean 'constancy and joy.'"

[1] John xv. 16.   [2] 1 John iv. 19.   [3] Prov. iv. 3.

"And," said Adolphe, "Evangelist and Evangeline must signify 'heralds of the Gospel;' Fidus must mean 'trusty;' Grace tells her own tale; Ruth, I think, means 'pity;' and Ancora, I suppose, stands for 'hope.' Did you mark, Aimée, how it was Ancora who tried to kindle Una's expectations of Shushan, and Ruth who told of the tender compassions of Adonais, and Grace against whom Una leaned when she yielded to the entreaties of Evangelist? Have the names Hammelech and Adonais any meaning, grandfather?"

"Yes," replied Oberlin. "Hammelech means 'the King,' and Adonais signifies 'Lord.'"

"And does Alp Arslan, the name of the rebel chief, mean any thing?" asked Gustave.

"Yes," said Oberlin, "Alp Arslan is the Saracen for 'a bold lion.'"

"Oh! then, of course," said Marie, "that is 'our adversary the devil, who goes about as a roaring lion, seeking whom he may devour.'[1] And I suppose the dreadful wound which Adonais received in battle with the foe is the serpent bruising the heel of the blessed Saviour on the cross."

"Quite right," said Oberlin; "and now that you have the right meaning of these names, and Sir John Davies's beautiful poem to help you, I think you hardly want any more aid from me to unlock every secret drawer of my cabinet, and to make all that is there your own. What I chiefly wanted you to learn from it was, how Jesus Christ wooes and wins the love of our hearts. His Gospel pleads for Him. His Spirit with all His tender graces urges His heavenly suit. He will take no denial. He knocks again and again at the door, till His people are made willing in the day of His power; and then, when they open the door, He comes in and betroths them to Himself in an everlasting covenant of love."

[1] 1 Peter v. 8.

"And yet, grandfather," said Aimée, "Una had a long, long time to wait, after she consented to become the bride of Adonais, before her marriage day."

"But the time was not lost, Aimée, was it?" rejoined Oberlin. "We too have a long while to wait after Jesus wins our hearts, before we see Him as He is and love Him as we ought. Or, if you interpret my parable of the whole church, Jesus betrothed her to Himself when He came the first time in great humility, and sent forth His ambassadors into all the world. Then the betrothal ring was put on her finger, and she was enriched with priceless jewels of His grace. But He went into a far country to receive for Himself a kingdom and to return. He is expecting until His foes are made His footstool. But, meanwhile, His church year by year is learning innumerable lessons, which will make her more fit to enter into His mind and share His throne for ever. She is suffering with Him now that she may reign with Him for ever. But, when His time is fully come, He will come again and receive her unto Himself, that where He is there she may be also."

"O grandfather," said Gustave, "I was so glad that Una did not altogether lose her native Eden by going to dwell at Shushan. But what does this mean? We cannot keep our earthly joys when we go to be with Jesus in heaven."

"Perhaps our next parable may tell us more of this, Gustave," answered Oberlin. "But, meanwhile, please read the first three verses of the twenty-first chapter of Revelation."

Gustave reads:— "And I saw a new heaven and a new earth, for the first heaven and the first earth were passed away, and there was no more sea. And I, John, saw the holy city, new Jerusalem, coming down from God out of heaven, prepared as a bride adorned for her husband. And I heard a great voice out of heaven, saying, Behold the tabernacle of God is with men, and He will dwell with them, and they shall be His people, and God Himself shall be with them and be their God."

"You see," said Oberlin, "there is a new earth as well as a new heaven, and these are for ever united in eternity. And as the parable tells of Una making her children princes in all lands, herein echoing the promise of the song of loves,[1] so we are assured, regarding the kingdom of our Emanuel, 'Of the increase of His government and peace there shall be no end.'[2] Only let us yield our hearts up to the messages of His love now, and when He brings us home to the many mansions of His Father, and makes us to inherit His everlasting kingdom, we, too, each one of us, shall say with the Queen of Sheba, 'The half was not told me.'"

[1] Psalm xlv. 16.   [2] Isa. ix. 7.

BEYOND THE RIVER.

NOT a shadow of a cloud flecked the mountains. The summer sun was setting and bathing in its pure amber light the vineyards and groves of arbutus through which the frontier river flowed between France and Switzerland; especially where, at the furthest extremity of a secluded valley, the river broadened into what were known as *Les Basses Terribles*, so named from many travellers having lost their lives in attempting to wade through the shallows, the roseate hues of evening were reflected as in a broad mirror to heaven. The valley, which was called at that time *Le Val de Grace*, though the name has long since passed away, was one of the most fertile in all France, and from its opening defile to the banks of the river, extended nearly twenty miles in length. But that river then flowed between the land of fiery persecution and the mountain fastnesses of truth and freedom.

Of that persecution my words here must be very few. Let it suffice to say that the soil of *la belle France*, from the English Channel to the Jura Alps, from the Rhine to the Pyrenees, was stained with the blood of tens of thousands of her noblest citizens, whose only crime was an invincible love for the pure word of life. The scourge and the sword spared neither men, nor women, nor children. A ferocious and pitiless soldiery was quartered in the homes of holy piety and peace. The iron entered into the souls of the sufferers. Hard as it was to tear themselves from the homesteads of their childhood and the graves of their forefathers, their only safety was in flight; and yet flight was sternly prohibited them under the rigid penalties of imprisonment and death. But inflexible conscience braved all this for the truth's sake. It was found quite impossible to guard so extensive a frontier as France. By unfrequented paths over the hills and through the forests, in the darkness of night, amid the snows of winter, under the cloak of mists, through the howling of the tempests, in rude rafts over the rivers and in open boats by sea, month after month, and year after year, the refugees made their escape from their unhappy and ungrateful fatherland. Other countries were as much enriched as France was drained by this exodus of the best and faithfullest of her children.

Le Val de Grace, lying so sequestered from the main courses of travel and of traffic, was one of the latest spots on which the storms of persecution fell, and hence it had been for many years a secret door of escape by which the refugees from other provinces, making their way across *Les Basses Terribles*, under the guidance of those who knew every shelving ledge of the river fords, had gained the free and friendly shore of Switzerland. Immediately on the other side of the river there was a small retired glen of singular beauty and fruitfulness, sheltered by precipitous rocks from every stormy blast, and the narrow entrance of which — so narrow that two could not walk abreast — was concealed by moss-grown rocks and overhanging trees. Here the refugees were accustomed to stay and refresh themselves for a while, until they had gained strength to go up to the city among the mountains. This city, Villafranca, or "the free city," as it was happily called after its Tuscan namesake by those who had escaped from a worse than Egyptian bondage, was rapidly rising in beauty and importance. Its situation was perfect. Built upon a fertile hill, through the vineyards of which flowed many springs of perennial water, it was itself embosomed by ranges of yet loftier mountains. Its inhabitants were either those who had suffered the loss of all things for the truth's sake, or the free-born natives of the hills, who had welcomed them as brothers to this asylum of liberty. Wherever you looked, the graceful skill and untiring industry of the citizens were apparent. There were gardens of delight attached to every home. The noble spires of that beautiful temple, where, Sabbath by Sabbath and day by day, they met to worship God, none making them afraid, pierced the deep blue sky. A massive wall surrounded the city, but the gates stood open night and day, for no foe dared to set his foot on that sacred soil. Switzerland was then, as now, Freedom's fortress. And the voice of song and the merry laughter of children were again heard in a thousand circles, from which innocent mirth had seemed for ever banished. The princely leader under whose banner they had fought had his mansion here, and it was open to all who chose to partake of his boundless hospitalities. And the unflagging object of interest was, who next of their friends or kindred should join them in this their new but delightful home.

I said that *Le Val de Grace* was one of the very last retreats on which persecution laid its cruel hands. But at length the tempest fell. And now for six weeks that smiling valley had been desolated with fire and sword. The vineyards were trampled down, the modest churches given to the flames, and the fairest homes polluted with bloodshed and violence. Wherever the marauding soldiers reached, when they went on their way it was as if a dreadful avalanche had passed over the loving labors of immemorial years.

How little nature seemed to reck of the disastrous deeds of man! The sun, as I said, was sinking in unclouded glory. There was not a shadow of mist upon the hills. The air was crystal. And through a gorge of the mountains the spires and turrets of Villafranca were easily discernible from the fords and far down the valley beyond. For the beauty and calm of the landscape it might have been what one has called "the sinless eve of a sinful world."

It was upon that lovely summer evening I was gazing upon the mingled topaz and ruby and emerald of the sky reflected in the tranquil waters of the fords; and my thoughts had wandered far away to the better land of promise, when I was startled by hearing the anxious and somewhat feeble tread of an old man approaching the river brink. He led by the hand a lovely child, on whose innocent face certainly not more than six summers had imprinted their kisses, and who with unequal paces tripped timidly beside him. When they came to the very edge of the ford, the old man, looking keenly around and seeing no one, took the child in his arms and pressed her to his heart, and said in a low voice, though every accent fell on my ear,

"Celeste, my pretty lamb, my blossom, I have shielded thee from a thousand dangers these last three weeks. The spoiler has not touched one of thy golden hairs. But, perhaps, the worst peril remains. I must bear thee, as best I may, over these treacherous shallows. I have never passed this way heretofore. Oh, would that the prince who knows every step of the river-bed were but here himself to bear his little foster-sister to his beautiful city garden! But we must not linger. May God protect us!"

As the old man spoke, he dipped the soles of his feet in the shallow water, and was about to wade into the stream, when a noble figure, muffled in a warrior's scarlet cloak, approached from behind, and laying a hand upon his shoulder said, "Stay, Pascal, I am here. Give me thy precious burden. It is not thy time to cross over yet. I have yet work for thee to do on this side the river. The two brothers of this innocent babe — though they have suffered and toiled far more than she whom thou hast borne in thine aged arms so many weary leagues — have, I know, hitherto escaped the sword of the foe. They too are making for these fords by many a perilous track. But they cannot now be so very far away. In a day, or two days at the longest, methinks they will be here. Pascal, wilt not thou for my sake and for the sake of Celeste, tarry on this side a little longer, and seek out Hilaire and Victor, and encourage them for this last trial of their faith? I will return and meet them at this spot, and when I have placed them in safety with this lamb, will conduct thee, their faithful and tender shepherd, over to our happy fold yonder. Be of good comfort. There are no troubles there."

The old man did not wait for the prince to finish his entreaty; but resigned his priceless charge to her foster-brother's clasp, and himself regained the shore. But whether it was that the chill of the waters that had flowed around his ankles produced a dizziness of brain, or whether the gorgeous sunset light upon the shallows into which the prince immediately waded dazzled him, or whether an intense craving to go with his little ewe lamb unnerved him for a few minutes, I know not. Certain it was, Pascal very soon lost sight both of the child and of the prince. But he thought he heard a voice which sounded far away over the waters, and it seemed to come from that radiant track they had trodden, "Good by — soon, very soon to meet again."

Then Pascal remembered the flask, containing a restorative cordial, which the prince had slipped into the bosom of his dress when they parted; and he drank of it, and was refreshed, and turned with new strength to seek for Hilaire and Victor.

Meanwhile, the prince, with Celeste in his arms, had waded two-thirds of the way across *Les Basses Terribles*. Even in the calmest weather, as that evening, the shallows were perilous, except to one who knew them well, by reason of the extreme unevenness of the river-bed. Now they would only reach to the knees, and a few feet further on the unwary traveller would find himself up to his armpits in water, or even out of his depth altogether. But so deftly did the prince pick his way through the mazes of the ford, that thus far he had not dipped even the skirt of Celeste's garment in the river. There remained, however, the deepest channel of the passage. The waters now washed his loins, and the rock still shelved downwards. Only saying to Celeste, " Throw your arms around my neck, darling, and fear nothing," he pressed on. For a few moments the gently rippling waves flowed over the slender form of the child as she clung to the prince, though he rather held her than she him; but the rays of the setting sun shone so brightly upon her clear blue eyes, not even a shudder passed through her tender limbs, nor did a sob rise to her lips. She only looked up into the prince's face and smiled. And now, for the water shoaled rapidly, he bore her quickly to the further brink of the river, and fervently exclaiming, "Here my lamb is safe," he carried her in his arms to the little glen of which I spoke before. Passing rapidly through the narrow entrance, three lovely maidens met him, robed in white, to one of whom he gave his little nursling, and she took Celeste and stripped her of her dripping garments and put on her shining apparel as pure as the driven snow, and led her among some playmates of her own age, who were singing in the purple twilight. But I could see no more by reason of the overhanging moss-grown rock and the bowering trees.

That night the storm clouds, which had been gathering unseen behind the mountains, broke in a tempest on the nearer hills. The blue lightnings seemed to open a pathway into the unutterable glory of the heavens. These were followed by drifts of impetuous rains. The water-courses were soon filled to their very brim. A thousand wayside brooklets filled the river, and the next morning *Les Basses Terribles* was one roaring, seething torrent from shore to shore. " Thank God," I said to myself, " Celeste is safe across the fords. How I wish I knew where Pascal was, and the two boys he went to seek!" I had not long to wait for tidings of them, for as I retraced my footsteps along *Le Val de Grace*, I saw Hilaire in the midst of a group of insolent and exultant soldiers. He was nearly twice the age of Celeste, and for precaution's sake, to avoid observation, he had travelled an altogether different track from that pursued by the aged Pascal and his little sister. He had chosen to thread the labyrinths of the vineyard paths; while Victor, who was two years older than himself, had taken the yet more difficult goat-tracks on the upper edge of the valley. Hilaire had escaped innumerable perils, which it were far too long here to narrate, and was pleasing himself with the thought that he was approaching the fords, for through the crystal atmosphere of yesterday, on every vantage-ground which the vineyards gave him, he had caught many a glimpse of Villafranca's walls and spires. But that stormful night had drenched him to the skin, and very early in the morning, observing a watch-fire burning in a forest, he had incautiously drawn near; and hearing a voice which he mistook for that of a friend, he approached the group which was gathered round the ruddy flame. In a moment he was seen and seized. Alas! his supposed friend had proved a traitor to the sacred cause of truth, and a guide to the cruel persecutors. Finding some leaves of the Gospel of St. John secreted in the bosom of the boy's dress, they sought no further witness against him, but loaded him with hard words and harder blows; and when the sun was up they placed him in their midst, and compelled him to march on with them, bruised and footsore as he was, goading him on with the points of their swords. My heart was sore within me to think of the poor lad's fate. But now the soldiers, having reached their mid-day halt, tied the hapless Hilaire hand and foot, with cords that lacerated his wrists and ankles, to the stump of a mountain ash, and having thrown their cloaks on the turf lay down to rest.

Then it was that I observed the aged Pascal, disguised as a shepherd, with his crook in hand and a skin bottle of wine slung over his shoulders, approaching them. Courteously saluting the soldiers, he offered them of the refreshing juice of the grape, and partook thereof himself, and afterwards cast himself on the ground beside them, apparently to rest. But no sooner were the men drenched in sleep than Pascal, noiselessly rising, stole to the side of Hilaire; and, touching the tort cords that bound him with the keen edge of his shepherd's knife, set him in a moment free. The poor lad would have fallen to the earth; but Pascal grasped him with a strength beyond his years, and half dragged, half carried him, for many hundred yards, up the channel of a noisy mountain stream which flowed hard by. Then, springing into a thicket, by a thousand intricate turns and windings he made his painful and perilous way towards the fords.

The soldiers soon woke, and, missing their prize, shouted and hissed for rage; but seeing no footprints save those on the path by which the shepherd had approached, they pursued the fugitives in vain; until at last, concluding the boy would certainly make for the fords, they bent their footsteps thither, if possible to intercept his flight. But when they reached a rising knoll which commanded a view of *Les Basses Terribles*, and saw the foaming waters which went eddying down the shallows, they did not care to approach nearer, arguing that no one could possibly cross that day.

Now Pascal and Hilaire had reached the river brink but a little before them, and had concluded to lie concealed among the osiers until the sudden flood had subsided. This, therefore, they did; and in truth the waters began to sink almost as rapidly as they had risen. And now the sun set fiery red, and the saffron twilight faded into darkness, till the crescent moon arose, and then Pascal ventured to sing in a low voice a few words of a hymn, which was the signal agreed upon. They were immediately answered from some clustering shrubs on the left, and the well-known and majestic form of the prince appeared quietly moving along the bank of the river.

Pressing his fingers upon his own lips in token of silence, the prince produced bread and wine from a wallet which he carried, by which, when the exhausted Pascal and Hilaire had partaken, they were greatly revived. But the time was short; and when the prince had whispered a few words in the ear of Pascal, the old man, silently wringing the hand of Hilaire, glided like a shadow himself away among the shadows of a rhododendron copse. He was soon lost from sight. And then the prince, taking Hilaire tenderly and firmly by the hand, said, " We must venture now; " and at the word they waded into the stream, which even a few yards from the shore was up to the prince's loins. Could they have waited six hours more, the fords would have regained their usual level. But it might not be. There was not a moment to be lost, for one of the soldiers, happening to look through the misty moonlight, saw one or more figures against the sheen of the water, and instantly gave the alarm to his comrades. They rushed down the declivity to the river's side, but by this time the prince and Hilaire had gained a tiny furze-grown islet, whose bushes, still dripping from the recent flood, afforded them for a few minutes a scant shelter from observation. But, the moon shining out from behind a cloud, the gleaming point of the prince's spear, which he used as a fording pole, revealed their retreat. And the soldiers, with a yell of vengeance, dashed into the ford in pursuit. Not knowing the track, the two foremost floundered unawares into a deep pit, called "the dead man's grave," and, weighed down with their armor, sank, with a cry of despair, to rise no more. This brought the others to a standstill; till at length some of them again took heart, and painfully groping their way every step, with many a curse on their lips, reached the islet. The rest regained the shore.

Meanwhile, the prince and Hilaire, whose joyous courage was raised to the highest pitch by the peril of the hour and the nearness of safety, had already traversed successfully more than half the passage. Little more than their heads now appeared above water, the prince grasping his spear with one hand and holding Hilaire round his waist with the other; but the soldiers on the islet, catching a glimpse of them by the struggling moonlight, discharged their arquebuses again and again. Those on the shore did likewise.

The heavy shot ploughed the water all around, but the glancing current deceived the aim of their pursuers, and only one bolt grazed the left hand of Hilaire as he snatched for support at a branch that floated by. Instantly the prince whispered in his ear, "Be of good cheer, Hilaire, we shall soon be out of their reach: the deepest channel is now before us; but trust to me;" and immediately grasping the boy with the strength of a giant, now wading, now standing tiptoe, and stemming the current on a narrow ledge of rock, now swimming for a few yards to the next resting-place, though sometimes for a few seconds the waters flowed over Hilaire's head, at last he buffeted his way to the further side. "All right now," said he; and Hilaire answered, "Yes, thanks to thee, my liege, all right."

Swiftly the prince bore him to the sheltered glen, whither he had borne Celeste. The warden of the entrance received the boy at his hands and tenderly dressed his wounds, and clothed him in beautiful apparel, and, when the morning broke over the mountains, led him to a happy group of children, of whom Celeste was the first to throw her little arms around his neck and sob for joy.

Now, when the aged Pascal had left Hilaire, he threaded his path through the shrubs and rocks, according to the prince's direction, to a ruined tower, which the enemy had consigned to the flames some little while before. It was built on a wooded ledge, half way up the cliff which formed the first ascent from the valley, but was now a roofless tenement, whose blackened rafters, as you gazed up at them from the blood-stained floor, intersected the sky like a gridiron. Here, crouching into an arch behind some twisted hinges which alone remained to tell an oaken door had once been there, Pascal lay and rested, half awake, half asleep, for three hours or more.

He was roused by the approach of footsteps and low suppressed voices. Yes, it was Victor, haggard and travel-worn, and weary with three weeks of privation and peril and pain; but in his eye a dauntless fire which told of what blood he sprang. Nor was he alone. He led by the hand a little orphan boy scarcely so old as Celeste, whose name was Theodore, and whom four days before he had found absolutely starving on the skirts of the forest. His parents, brothers, and sisters had been ruthlessly murdered, and he only had escaped the merciless foe in the confusion. Victor, who was himself hiding in the wood, heard a child's voice feebly moaning, "Our Father which art in heaven." He instantly went to the boy's side, and broke into his lips the last crust, which was all that he had for his own food that day. Then, emerging from the wood at the risk of his life, he plucked some grapes that hung over the wall of a neighboring vineyard, and filled his leathern cup from a babbling stream, and brought them wearily to little Theodore. How his heart danced for joy to see the color coming back to the child's white lips, and the light to his large black eyes! And how instinctively he vowed in his heart that he would never leave that innocent babe to perish!

Victor kept his vow, but it cost him dear. Things he could have dared and done, and would have dared and done without a second thought when alone, he could not dream of attempting with that little orphan clinging about his feet. They were sorely pinched with hunger: but once, when they were at the worst, a goat suffered Victor to approach her and milk into his leathern cup a draught of milk, in the strength of which they went for hours. Often they were within a hair's-breadth of discovery; and once, when lying beneath some newly mown grass, felt the ground tremble beneath the tread of a file of soldiers who passed within three feet of that ditch in which they lay. But God shielded them. During all that stormy night Theodore lay in Victor's bosom, who bent over him hour after hour like the tenderest nurse, and kept warmth in his drenched limbs. And in the glow of the next evening the prince (it must have been an hour or so before he answered Pascal's signal by the river bank) came to them, when lurking in the hollow of an old yew-tree, and almost strengthless for want of food, and fed them with his own hands and cheered them on, assuring Victor that even with the care of little Theodore, by a rugged upland path of which he told them, they might reach the ruined tower overlooking the fords of which I spoke before daybreak, that there they should find Pascal, and that he himself would meet them by the river side, and conduct them in safety over the waters.

These, then, were the footsteps and these the voices which roused the half slumbers of Pascal. As they crept into the ruined tower, they passed his archway lair, and the old man at once recognized Victor and softly called him by his name. In another moment the youth was in his arms, and drew Theodore to him for his blessing. But they had no time to lose. There was already the faintest streak of opal light in the eastern sky. So the old man and the boys silently stole down the side of the cliff by a goat path known to very few, and when they reached the bottom, now crouching among the ferns, now pressing on through copses and brakes, at length they stood undiscovered under the shadow of the river bank on the very brink of the fords. They had scarcely time to look around, when they saw the prince coming not fifty paces from them through the shallows. He warmly saluted them, and smiled with a smile of delighted majesty as Victor led Theodore to his feet. He laid his hands upon them all, and then calmly said, " The fords have sunk to their summer level. One journey across will suffice. You, Pascal, take Theodore in your arms, and I will hold you with my right hand and Victor with my left. The foe will not be astir for another hour. There is no danger in this early twilight."

And so it came to pass. Without haste or even a shadow of fear they quietly and trustfully made their way over *Les Basses Terribles*, sweetly conversing in the water of the manifold providences which had attended them, and of the happy reunion with long-parted friends which was before them. As they stepped on the further shore, the first ray of the rosy sun lighted up the snowy locks of the aged Pascal, till they shone like a crown of glory.

The prince quickly led them to the sequestered glen, which now sheltered so many rescued ones. Their dripping garments were all exchanged for comely apparel from his royal wardrobe, for he was pleased to keep a supply of vestments always there, and then they went further into the glen. And I heard a shout of glee from the children, and thought I distinguished the soft, clear voices of Celeste and Hilaire, who had only shortly before found each other, exclaiming, "And here's Victor! And here's Pascal, and a boy in his arms! And oh, here's the prince!"

As I just glanced up and down that glen, it seemed to me a perfect little paradise, embracing in itself every thing for refreshment and repose. There were fruit-trees of all kinds, and mossy banks, and arbors, and streams of crystal water. But I could not see so much as I wished that morning, for my eyes swam so with tears of tenderness and gratitude, it almost seemed to me as if there was a veil over them.

Seven happy days passed like dreams of delight, during which the children and Pascal lost every sense of fatigue and trace of suffering. And then it was rumored that the prince intended to take them and the other travellers who had gathered there in his royal chariots to the mountain city, the new and beautiful metropolis, Villafranca. So, very early on the morrow morning there was

a throng of chariots and a brave retinue of attendants, who waited all along the river banks by the entrance of the glen. The prince was now by the side of one, and now by the side of another. He had a word and a smile for every one. His presence was sunshine.

But time would utterly fail me to sketch, however briefly, the past history of all those pilgrims, or their joyous ascent that day through the mountains, which echoed to their mirth and the songs of the charioteers, or their peaceful entrance within the walls of their city. Besides, I kept my eye especially upon Celeste and Hilaire, and Victor and Theodore and Pascal. They filled one chariot; and the prince blessed each and all of them as he passed on to the head of the procession, and bade them be sure and follow him, even to his royal palace.

And now right rapidly they moved onward through the fresh, balmy air. The air was filled with the melody of sweet voices uttering joy. Most delightful was the converse they held with the royal servants who had come from the city to attend them. With Pascal especially the ministering couriers were graciously familiar, and he communicated all he learned to the children. And every thing he told them awoke hallelujahs in their hearts, which often sprang unbidden to their lips.

When they were within a mile of the city gates a large multitude of the citizens came forth to meet them, with garlands and banners and trumpets, and all instruments of music, and every sign which could testify how joyfully they welcomed them. It is quite impossible to tell the story of the meetings which took place that day of those who had parted from each other in pain and peril. Let it suffice to say, that as the mingled throng entered the open portals, the earth rang again, and again, and yet again, to their loud and persistent acclamations.

Pascal and the little group of those he

loved to call his children at length arrived at the mansions of the royal palace. The prince was there to welcome them at the door; and when they passed into the hall of audience, lo, he was there on the throne. And he gave each one a token of his princely favor; to one a robe curiously inwrought with his name, to another a signet ring, to another a wand of office set with jewels. He himself entwined a garland of pearls among the beautiful ringlets of Celeste, and fastened his likeness with a chain of gold around the neck of Victor.

And then he led them into his banqueting-hall, and himself assigned them an honorable place at his table, and heaped the board with the choicest viands. So hour after hour passed away; until, after much precious converse with him and with each other, they passed forth to observe the marvels of the city.

One thing I took especial notice of, namely, that whatever Pascal, or Victor, or Hilaire, or even little Celeste or Theodore, had taken chief delight in when they dwelt in their native valley, *Le Val de Grace*, they found the same pleasure here in Villafranca, the city of the free, only in a purer form and a far higher degree. But to name a few examples out of many: how they loved their modest home in the valley, their nest, they called it; now this taste was gratified; they had a mansion assigned them which was part of the wing of the royal palace, but was yet peculiarly their own. One of Victor's choicest pleasures had always been his garden; and here there was an Eden in the very heart of the city. Hilaire's passion was music: here it seemed that every one could play well on an instrument, and every one could sing. Celeste's delight had often been in watching the shepherd leading his sheep and lambs through the green pastures of the valley; here it often seemed to her, as the prince led them forth and explained his thoughts and purposes towards his people, that she and her brother were the lambs and the prince himself the shepherd.

But their chiefest joy, as they agreed with common consent, was the Sabbath-day in Villafranca. Here it was a rest indeed, unbroken by any thought of the foe. Here the happy family circles or groups of friends met together to study the pages of truth or sing their hymns, none making them afraid. And here were their holy convocations in that beautiful temple which was the glory of all that land, and their solemn feasts of love, and those magnificent anthems in which thousands of voices joined in thanking God for their freedom and felicity in the happy city of the free.

"DEAR, dear master," exclaimed Marie, with her eyes brimming over with tears, which coursed one another down her wrinkled cheeks, "did not all that really happen now? I feel sure it did. I've heard my old father tell what he heard from his mother's mother, who fled herself with her three little pitiful bairns from beautiful France across the river Doubs into Switzerland; and I am sure some of the things you said might have been taken down from his blessed lips."

"Well, Marie," answered Oberlin, while he brushed an answering tear from his own eye, "my tale was a parable. You must not question its history too closely. And yet you must forgive it, if it roots itself in fact, which is often stranger than fiction. I believe that some of our Divine Master's matchless parables, like the Good Samaritan and the Rich Man and Lazarus, were based on things which had recently occurred. But oh, how poor all other parables are to His!"

"I feel they are very different, grandfather," said Gustave; "but in what way are they so much poorer?"

"In every way," replied Oberlin. "Take

one for example. Here have I been reading you thirty closely written pages, and we have perhaps caught some glimpses of the passage over the river which flows betwixt us and the land of perfect freedom; but our Master, sometimes in a verse or two, as in the parable of the hidden Treasure, or the Pearl of great price, or sometimes in a few verses, as in the Ten Virgins, or the Vine and its branches, makes the whole truth live before you, crystal clear, and speak with you ever after, like a friend or a brother. I often think, when comparing man's words with God's, of what John Newton said about books. Some, he used to say, were all good enough in their way; but there was so little truth in so many pages; they were so bulky, it was like filling your pockets with copper money, very heavy and of small value. Others, he said, were better; they had more truth in less space, and they were like silver. And there were a few others better still, very choice books of rare value; they were like gold. But, he said, there was one book of which every leaf was a bank-note of inestimable worth: and that book was the Bible. However, I shall be quite content if my grandchildren can carry away with them in the silken purse of their memory a few silver coins from listening to my parable, '*Beyond the River.*'"

"I know, grandfather," said Adolphe, "that when you spoke of persecution making *Le Val de Grace* utterly desolate and spoiling its loveliest homes with fire and sword, you said nothing but what really happened to our ancestors; for I have been reading the history of the Huguenots till my cheeks burned and tingled. In those awful dragonnades, the soldiers seemed to stop at nothing. They were like blood-hounds let loose. And you have taught us that in a parable we must not expect every part to fit into the lesson it teaches. But if, as I suppose, that valley, when the persecution at length reached it and the people had to fly for their lives, signifies our pilgrim state here on earth, surely in happy England, and in days of peace like ours, we are not exposed to quite such great dangers, are we?"

"I grant you, my boy," answered Oberlin, "that as to things seen and temporal, our state now is rather described by St. Luke, when he said, 'Then had the churches rest throughout all Judea, and Galilee, and Samaria, and were edified; and walking in the fear of the Lord, and in the comfort of the Holy Ghost, were multiplied.'[1] Thank God for it! But looking at things unseen and eternal, we must remember that, taken at the best, this is a sin-stricken, death-stricken world. 'Sin entered into the world, and death by sin.'[2] And, as we saw with Avehdah, the land was as the garden of Eden before them, and behind them a desolate wilderness. No home is too lovely for sin and death to spoil. And there is a true sense in which every Christian pilgrim hears and

[1] Acts ix. 31. [2] Rom. v. 12.

obeys the command, 'Arise ye and depart, for this is not your rest: because it is polluted, it shall destroy you, even with a sore destruction.'[1] Those who are most anxious to remain here find it cannot be. Here we have no continuing city. Our days on the earth are as a shadow, and there is none abiding. But I allow the main drift of my parable pointed to crossing the river, and reaching first the glen, and afterwards going up to the city."

"Grandfather," exclaimed little Röschen, eagerly, "you said half a text which I found out just now. May I read it all? 'For here have we no continuing city, but we seek one to come.'[2] When you spoke of that city among the hills, I thought of my favorite hymn,

> 'Jerusalem, my happy home,
> Name ever dear to me.'

Oh, how I wish we could really see its walls and spires from this valley!"

[1] Micah ii. 10.   [2] Heb. xiii. 14.

"Why," chimed in Gustave, "if only we could see Bunyan's Celestial City, I don't think I should trouble about any thing that lay betwixt us and it. But, Röschen, dear, you and I must remember what grandfather said about being willing to walk by faith and not by sight."

"Yes, my boy," said Oberlin, and his happy smile told how his heart rejoiced that Gustave was learning this lesson, "and we do see Jerusalem the Golden by the eye of faith. Faith is the soul's eye. And so we read, shortly before the text Röschen quoted, that the pilgrim fathers, who confessed that they were strangers here, and were seeking a heavenly fatherland, 'looked for a city which hath foundations, whose builder and maker is God.'[1] Its glory shines right down the valley of life to the farthest narrow entrance; even children may catch many a glimpse of it. But it ought to attract the eye and fill the heart far more as the traveller draws nearer and nearer

[1] Heb. xi. 10.

the brink of the river fords. Those fords, *Les Basses Terribles* of our parable, must be crossed by all."

" Little Celeste did not find them terrible, grandfather, did she?" asked Aimée. " I envied her, led to the very banks of the river by her dear old pastor, who had shielded her from every danger, so that he said no one had touched one of her golden hairs, and then gently placed her in the prince's arms, who carried her over so tenderly that she never even shuddered when the waters flowed over her. O, I should like to cross the river so!"

"And yet," broke in old Robin, " if I read the meaning right, thousands and thousands of infant children do die, and know nothing about it, till they are carried right into heaven by the Good Shepherd."

" And not babes in years only," replied Oberlin, "but young men and maidens, aye, and old saints too, who have a child's heart and a child's faith, pass over to the better land without a shadow of a cloud of fear, though sometimes, I know, the waters are far deeper than at others."

"Why did the story make," asked Röschen, "Pascal so soon lose sight of Celeste and the prince? I think it would have cheered the old man so, if he could have seen them step upon the opposite bank."

"Ah, my lamb," answered Oberlin, "friends may come with us to the river brink, but they cannot go over themselves till their own time is come; and often they cannot see to the further side, though a smile on the cheek and a light in the eye tell of the glory which the dying saint is entering. It is the office of the chief shepherd only, who knows every step of the passage, — for He once forded it in the days of His flesh, — to be with us in crossing *Les Basses Terribles.* Can you tell me any Scriptures which speak of this?"

"My psalm," replied Röschen, "says, 'Yea, though I walk through the valley of the shadow of death, I will fear no evil, for

Thou art with me.'[1] Only there it is a valley, and not a river."

"But in Isaiah we find the very figure of our parable," said Aimée. "'When thou passest through the waters I will be with thee, and through the rivers, they shall not overflow thee.'"[2]

"And I thought," said Adolphe, "of the children of Israel passing over Jordan, and of the words of Joshua, 'Behold the ark of the covenant of the Lord of all the earth passeth over before you into Jordan;'[3] and you remember, when the feet of the priests that bore the ark were dipped in the brim of the water, the river was divided, and the people passed over dry-shod. Only then it was so different from the prince himself wading through the waters, and carrying the pilgrims in his arms, or holding them by their hand while they crossed."

"But at least," said Oberlin, "the history of Israel may tell us that when we have

---

[1] Psalm xxiii. 4.   [2] Isa. xliii. 2.   [3] Josh. iii. 2.

walked through the weary wilderness, there yet flows the Jordan between us and Canaan, and how blessed they are who have an Incarnate Saviour, of whom the ark was a type, with them. Terrible, indeed, must be the passage of the river of death for those who have no Almighty Friend to meet them there."

"May I make so bold, sir, as to ask," said Robin, "what the tempest which broke over the mountains and swelled the fords so terribly signifies? My heart almost misgave me for that poor lad, Hilaire."

"Many things may make death more fearful to some Christians than to others," answered Oberlin. "Sometimes their bodily sufferings are very great; sometimes the memory of past sins, even though they have all been washed away in Christ's blood, seems almost to overwhelm the mind; sometimes Satan is permitted to aim many a fiery dart at the trembling traveller, as he is buffeting his way through the waters. But if the

Prince is with him, and holds him fast, all is well, for no one has ever yet plucked one of His sheep or lambs out of the arms of the Good Shepherd. Hilaire got over as safely, though not so smoothly, as Celeste."

"And then," said Adolphe, "how perfectly delightful it must have been for Victor to rescue that little Theodore. Oh! I think of all joys in the world, the greatest must be to save a soul from death. Is there any meaning in the goat-tracks on the upper edge of the valley being so dangerous, grandfather?"

"Perhaps we might say," answered Oberlin, "that those who tread the heights of thought are exposed most to rocks and precipices, as well as other perils. But we must hasten on to consider their happy lot beyond the river. They all got safely over under the guidance and guardianship of the prince. What do you understand by the sheltered glen on the further side?"

"Oh, grandfather," said Aimée, "is it not

that paradise of which you so often speak to us, where our dear father and mother, and all who sleep in Jesus, are?"

"Then I suppose the three maidens who took Celeste were angels," said Röschen.

"And the fruit-trees and the rivulets of that glen, and the meadows where the children played, would, I suppose," said Gustave, "answer to the heavenly pleasures of those of whom we read that the Lamb which is in the midst of the throne shall feed them, and lead them to living fountains of water.[1] How my heart leaped up with them when Celeste and Hilaire sprang to welcome Victor and Pascal and the prince! I wish the one who spoke of what he saw in the glen that morning had not so dimmed his eyes with tears that he could not see clearly. He seemed to know more about the city than the glen."

"And the Bible," said Oberlin, "tells us more about the New Jerusalem than it does about the paradise of the blessed dead.

[1] Rev. vii. 17.

However, it tells us quite enough for us to know that happy as it is to serve Christ here, whom not having seen we love, it will be far happier to go and be with Him whom our soul loveth, and with all those who have crossed over the river before us in His faith and fear. To depart and be with Christ is far better.[1] It is, as He promised to the dying thief, to be with Him in paradise.[2] It is that state of which St. Paul wrote, 'We are confident and willing rather to be absent from the body and to be present with the Lord.'[3] It is the felicity of those of whom the voice from heaven spoke to St. John in Patmos, 'Blessed are the dead which die in the Lord,' and of whom the Spirit immediately bore witness, 'Yea, that they may rest from their labors; and their works do follow them,'[4] so that we may always think of the Christian's course as *good, better, best.* It is *good* to serve so dear a Master here: His

---

[1] Phil. i. 21.   [2] Luke xxiii. 43.
[3] 2 Cor. v. 8.   [4] Rev xiv. 13.

work is wages. It will be *better*, yes, *far better*, when He summons us to His presence and His rest with all the other holy dead. It will be *best of all* in the glory of the Resurrection morning, when we enter into the gates of the celestial city with everlasting joy upon our heads. Our parable did not stop short of this superlative joy."

"Oh, no, grandfather," said Gustave, "that procession from the glen to the city was so delightful. Of course we all thought of the close of the Pilgrim's Progress. Only there the pilgrims went straight up out of the river to the city which was builded higher than the clouds. I suppose by the chariots with their charioteers you meant angels; for I remembered the text, 'The chariots of God are twenty thousand, even thousands of angels,'[1] and how Lazarus was carried by the angels to Abraham's bosom."[2]

"And then," continued Adolphe, "the prince being with them, and having a word

[1] Psalm lxviii. 17.   [2] Luke xvi. 22.

and a smile for each, reminded me of the promise of Jesus: 'If I go and prepare a place for you, I will come again and receive you unto myself, that where I am there ye may be also.'[1] Surely this will be heaven's joy of joys."

"And how pleasant it must have been," cried Röschen, "for each of them to have received a gift from the prince's own hands! I think I should have liked the pearls best, they are so pure and lovely."

"Nay," said Aimée, "nothing could be so dear as the prince's own likeness. But I suspect they each thought their own the best, because it was his choice for them. Do you not think that the wand of office would be given to the beloved old Pascal, and the signet ring to Hilaire?"

"At all events," answered Oberlin, "the promise, 'Behold I come quickly, and my reward is with me to give every man according as his work shall be,'[2] assures us that no

[1] John xiv. 3.   [2] Rev. xxii. 12.

faithful laborer will be forgotten in that day. And then they all sat down to the banquet, and were all served by the prince himself. May not this remind us, that while some of the gifts of God's love in heaven are peculiar to each saint who receives them, many, perhaps most, of the joys of glory will be shared in common by all?"

"Oh, grandfather," said Gustave, "I was so very glad they found again in the city all the pleasures they had enjoyed in the valley, only so much more enjoyable than ever. The heaven which some persons describe seems so dull and so very different from that heaven you always lead us to expect."

"Well, dear boy," answered Oberlin, "let the Bible always decide these questions: for 'Eye hath not seen, nor ear heard, neither have entered into the heart of man, the things which God hath prepared for them that love Him; but God hath revealed them to us by His Spirit, for the Spirit searcheth all things, even the deep things of God.'[1] Does not the Bible speak of our dwelling hereafter in mansions, which shall be part of the royal palace?"

"Yes," said Gustave; "Jesus said, 'In my Father's house are many mansions; I go to prepare a place for you.'"[2]

"And of gardens of delight?" continued Oberlin.

"Yes," replied Adolphe; "'He showed me a pure river of water of life, clear as crystal, proceeding out of the throne of God and of the Lamb: in the midst of the street of it, and on either side of the river, was there the tree of life, which bare twelve manner of fruits, and yielded her fruit every month.'"[3]

"And of music, Aimée?" asked Oberlin.

"Yes, grandfather; St. John writes, 'I looked, and lo, a Lamb stood on the Mount Zion, and with Him an hundred forty and four thousand, having his Father's name

[1] 1 Cor. ii. 9, 10.   [2] John xiv. 2.   [3] Rev. xxii. 1, 2.

written in their foreheads. And I heard a voice from heaven, as the voice of many waters, and as the voice of a great thunder: and as the voice of harpers harping with their harps: and they sang as it were a new song before the throne.'"[1]

"And what did the text you repeated to me this morning tell of the Lord Jesus, shepherding His flock hereafter, Röschen?" said Oberlin.

"'Other sheep I have, which are not of this fold: them also I must bring, and they shall hear my voice; and there shall be one fold, and one shepherd,'"[2] answered Röschen.

"And lastly, does the Bible say any thing of temple worship?" asked Oberlin.

"Yes, grandfather," replied Adolphe, "we read of the white robed multitude, 'Therefore are they before the throne of God, and serve Him day and night in His temple.'"[3]

"God only grant," said the old man, fer-

[1] Rev. xiv. 1-3. [2] John x. 16. [3] Rev. vi. 15.

vently, "that we all, you my grandchildren, and you Marie, and you Robin, and all we love, may be among that blessed company of all faithful people who swell the tide of hallelujah before that throne, singing, 'Unto Him that loved us and washed us from our sins, and hath made us kings and priests unto God and His Father, to Him be glory and dominion for ever and ever. Amen.'"

Cambridge: Press of John Wilson & Son.

www.ingramcontent.com/pod-product-compliance
Lightning Source LLC
Chambersburg PA
CBHW021158230426
43667CB00006B/461